I0005228

Agile Project Management Training

Simple Kanban for Software Development Teams

Implementing Kanban using Scrum and other Agile techniques

Part of the Agile Education Series™

Copyright Notice 2015.

- This manual contains material copyrighted by Cape Project Management, Inc.

- All other brand or product names used in this guide are trade names or registered trademarks of their respective owners.

- Portions of this deck are based upon Open Kanban content, an open source Kanban approach (http://agilelion.com/agile-kanban-cafe/open-kanban) and is licensed under a Creative Commons Attribution 3.0 Unported license (http://creativecommons.org/licenses/by/3.0/)

- This presentation is based upon a blog post by Dan Tousignant:
  - http://www.agileprojectmanagementtraining.com/are-you-implementing-scrum-but-realize-you-are-better-suited-for-kanban/

2

Copyrighted material. 2015

Agile Project Management Training

Agile Ice Breaker

http://bit.ly/AgileGames

Copyrighted material. 2015

Agile Project
Management Training

3

Notes:

Introductions and Expectations

Copyrighted material. 2015

4

Agile Project
Management Training

Notes:

About Us

- The course curriculum developed by Dan Tousignant, PMI-ACP, CSP of Cape Project Management, Inc.
- We provide public, onsite and online training:
  - AgileProjectManagementTraining.com
- Follow us on Twitter @ScrumDan

- The content of this course is licensed to your instructor. You may purchase copies of this participant guide at:
  - http://bit.ly/DansAgileBooks

5

Copyrighted material. 2015

Agile Project Management Training

Notes:

Course Objectives

- Provide an in-depth training on Kanban best practices
- Learn what other Agile practices work well with Kanban
- Provide you with the knowledge and tools for you to go back and train your teams
- Have fun!

6

Copyrighted material. 2015

 Agile Project Management Training

Notes:

Agenda

Day 1	Day 2
Why Agile?	The Kanban Game
The Agile Manifesto	The Agile Product Lifecycle
Agile Approaches	Agile Controls
Simple Kanban	Implementing Kanban

7

Copyrighted material. 2015

 *Agile Project Management Training*

Notes:

Announcements

- Participant materials
  - Slides
  - Exercises
- Facilities orientation
- Breaks
- Emergencies

8

Copyrighted material. 2015

 Agile Project Management Training

Notes:

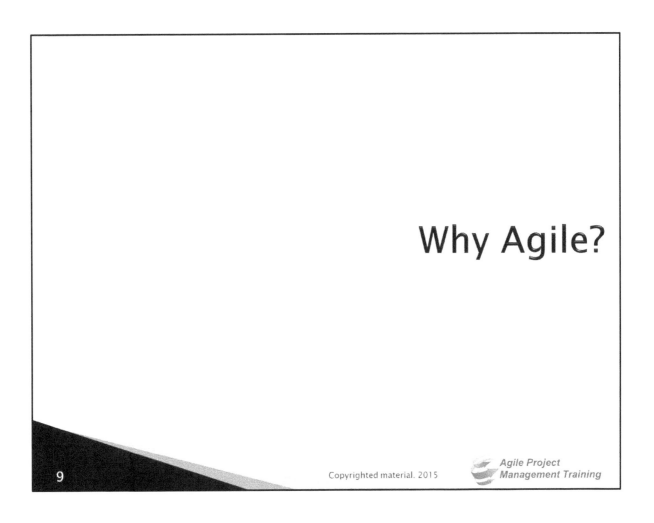

Copyrighted material. 2015

Agile Project Management Training

9

Notes:

Why Agile is so Successful

- Allows for more flexibility in requirements and development
- Promotes frequent releases
- Provides the opportunity to encounter and address errors sooner in the development cycle
- Increases organizational and team efficiency
- Decreases unnecessary documentation and meetings
- Provides a value-based approach to development
- Assumes organizational differences – can be right sized

10

Copyrighted material. 2015

 Agile Project Management Training

Notes:

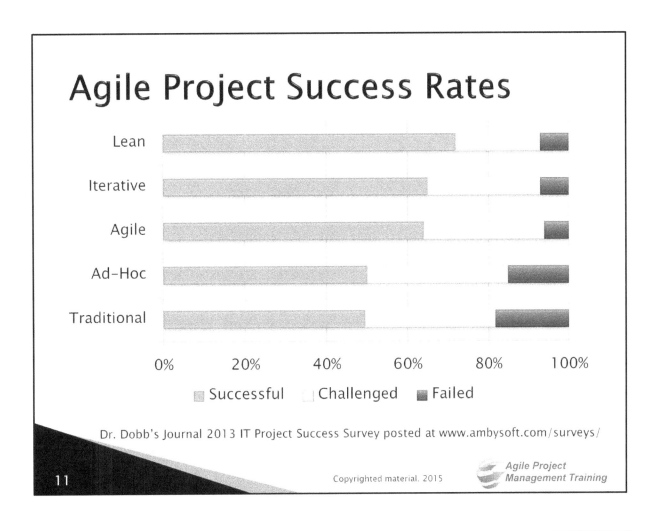

Requirements Stability vs. Development Approach

- Agile methods are often characterized as being at the opposite end of a spectrum from "plan-driven" or "disciplined" methodologies.
- This distinction is misleading, as it implies that Agile methods are "unplanned" or "undisciplined."
- It is more accurate to say that methods exist on a continuum from "adaptive" to "predictive." Agile methods exist on the "adaptive" side of this continuum.

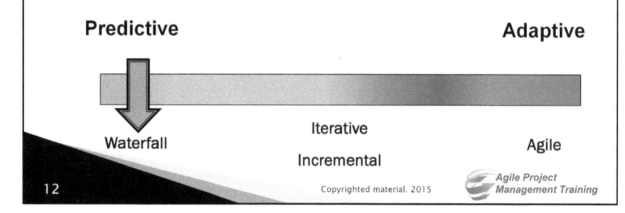

Predictive   **Adaptive**

Waterfall

Iterative

Incremental

Agile

Copyrighted material. 2015

Agile Project
Management Training

12

Notes:

Requirements Stability vs. Development Approach

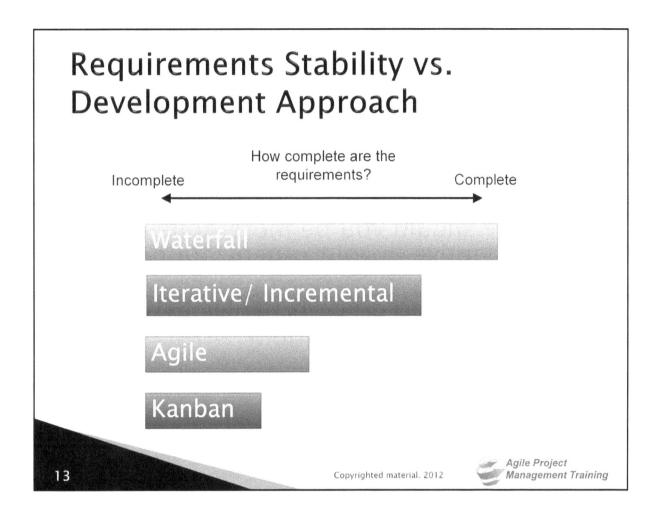

Copyrighted material. 2012

Agile Project Management Training

13

Notes:

Discussion

Why should you be more Agile or adaptive in your organization?

How do requirements evolve in your organization?

14

Copyrighted material. 2015

Agile Project
Management Training

Notes:

The Agile Manifesto

Copyrighted material. 2015

Agile Project
Management Training

15

Notes:

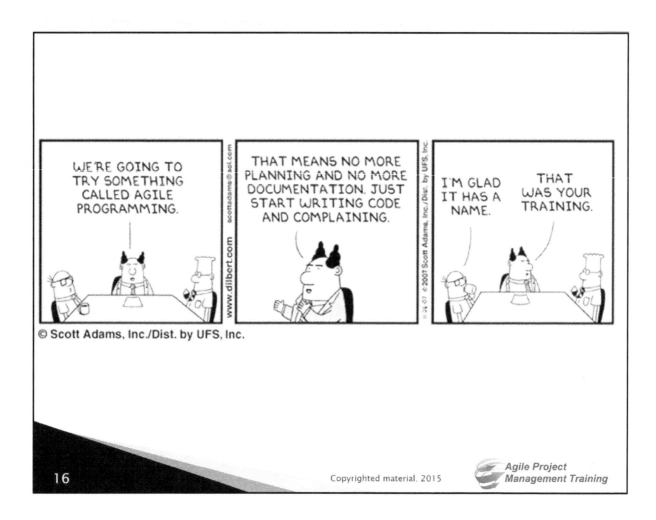

© Scott Adams, Inc./Dist. by UFS, Inc.

Copyrighted material. 2015

Agile Project Management Training

Notes:

The Agile Manifesto—a statement of values

Individuals and interactions	over	Process and tools
Working software	over	Comprehensive documentation
Customer collaboration	over	Contract negotiation
Responding to change	over	Following a plan

Source: www.agilemanifesto.org

Copyrighted material. 2015

Agile Project Management Training

17

Notes:

Twelve Principles of the Agile Manifesto

1. Our highest priority is to satisfy the customer through early and continuous delivery of valuable software.
2. Welcome changing requirements, even late in development. Agile processes harness change for the customer's competitive advantage.
3. Deliver working software frequently, from a couple of weeks to a couple of months, with a preference to the shorter timescale.
4. Business people and developers must work together daily throughout the project.
5. Build projects around motivated individuals. Give them the environment and support they need, and trust them to get the job done.
6. The most efficient and effective method of conveying information to and within a development team is face-to-face conversation.

18

Copyrighted material. 2015

Agile Project Management Training

Notes:

Twelve Principles of the Agile Manifesto

7. Working software is the primary measure of progress.

8. Agile processes promote sustainable development. The sponsors, developers, and users should be able to maintain a constant pace indefinitely.

9. Continuous attention to technical excellence and good design enhances agility.

10. Simplicity--the art of maximizing the amount of work not done--is essential.

11. The best architectures, requirements, and designs emerge from self-organizing teams.

12. At regular intervals, the team reflects on how to become more effective, then tunes and adjusts its behavior accordingly.

19

Copyrighted material. 2015

Agile Project Management Training

Notes:

Group Exercise

Your 3 Principles

Copyrighted material. 2015

Agile Project
Management Training

Notes:

Activity: Agile Manifesto Principles

Directions:

1. Pair-up with another person at your table and review the Agile Manifesto Principles.
2. Pick three principles that you think are critical to the success of your Agile Implementation or are the most challenging.
3. Be prepared to share your answer with the class.

Principle	Choose 3
1. Our highest priority is to satisfy the customer through early and continuous delivery of valuable software.	
2. Welcome changing requirements, even late in development. Agile processes harness change for the customer's competitive advantage.	
3. Deliver working software frequently, from a couple of weeks to a couple of months, with a preference to the shorter timescale.	
4. Business people and developers must work together daily throughout the project.	
5. Build projects around motivated individuals. Give them the environment and support they need, and trust them to get the job done.	
6. The most efficient and effective method of conveying information to and within a development team is face-to-face conversation.	
7. Working software is the primary measure of progress.	

©2015 Cape Project Management, Inc.

8. Agile processes promote sustainable development. The sponsors, developers, and users should be able to maintain a constant pace indefinitely.	
9. Continuous attention to technical excellence and good design enhances agility.	
10. Simplicity--the art of maximizing the amount of work not done--is essential.	
11. The best architectures, requirements, and designs emerge from self-organizing teams.	
12. At regular intervals, the team reflects on how to become more effective, then tunes and adjusts its behavior accordingly.	

Notes:

_____

_____

_____

_____

_____

_____

©2015 Cape Project Management, Inc.

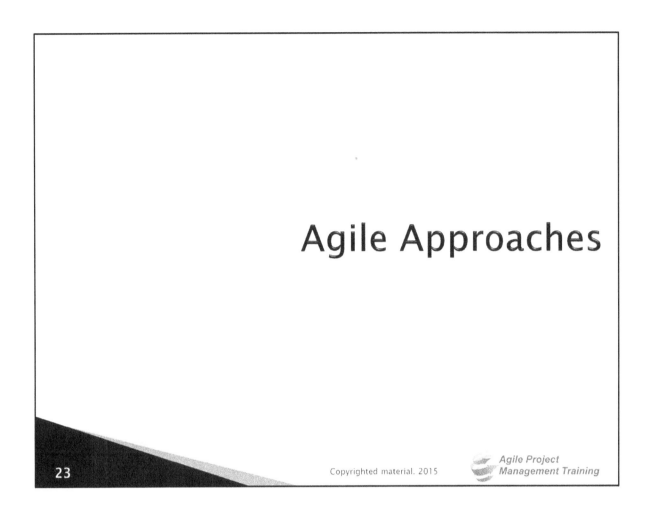

Agile Approaches

Copyrighted material. 2015

Agile Project
Management Training

23

Notes:

Agile Project Management

- There are many Agile approaches
- Agile as an umbrella term that encompasses other processes and practices, such as Scrum, Extreme Programming, Adaptive System Development, DSDM, Feature Driven Development, Kanban, Crystal and more...

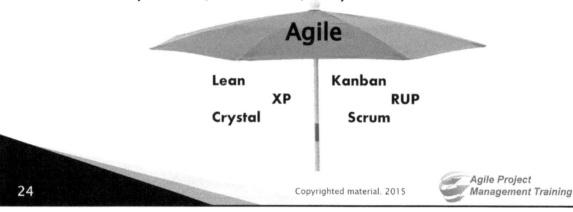

24

Copyrighted material. 2015

Agile Project Management Training

Notes:

| |
| |
| |
| |
| |
| |
| |
| |

Agile Approach Adoption

Scrum is by far the most widely adopted Agile approach.

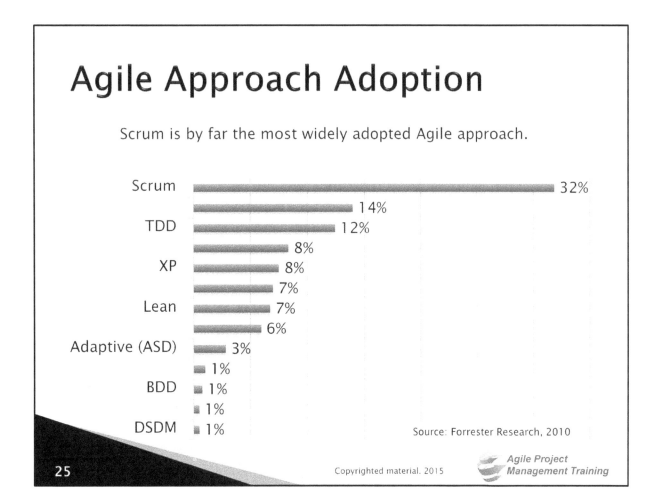

Source: Forrester Research, 2010

Copyrighted material. 2015

25

Agile Project Management Training

Notes:

Scrum Project Management

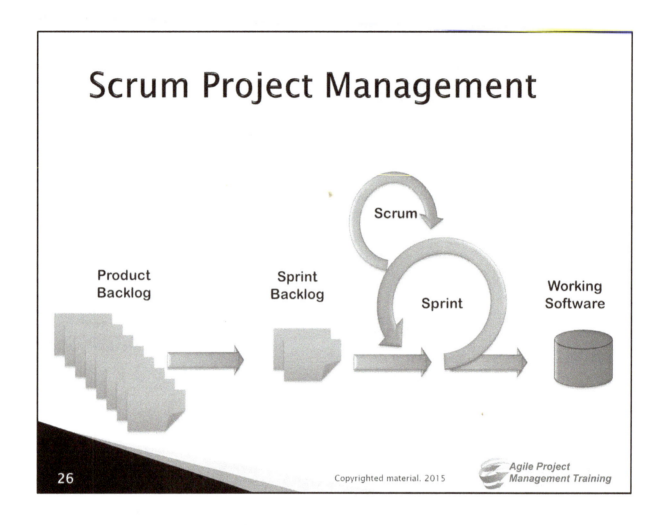

26

Copyrighted material. 2015

Agile Project
Management Training

Notes:

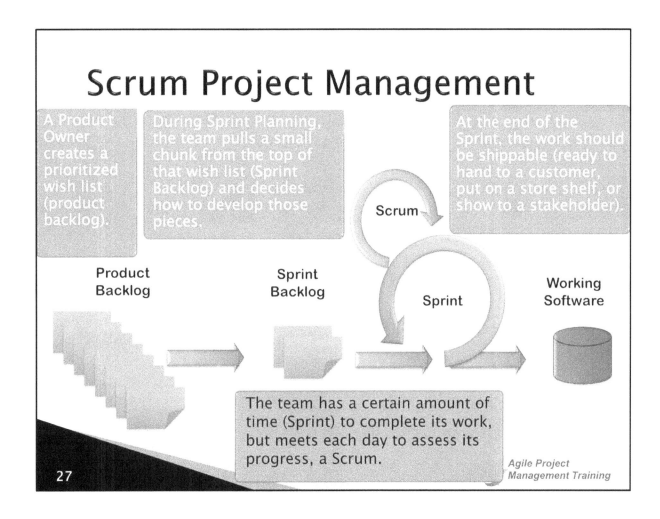

Scrum Project Management

A Product Owner creates a prioritized wish list (product backlog).

During Sprint Planning, the team pulls a small chunk from the top of that wish list (Sprint Backlog) and decides how to develop those pieces.

At the end of the Sprint, the work should be shippable (ready to hand to a customer, put on a store shelf, or show to a stakeholder).

Scrum

Sprint

Product Backlog

Sprint Backlog

Working Software

The team has a certain amount of time (Sprint) to complete its work, but meets each day to assess its progress, a Scrum.

Agile Project Management Training

27

Notes:

Extreme Programming (XP)

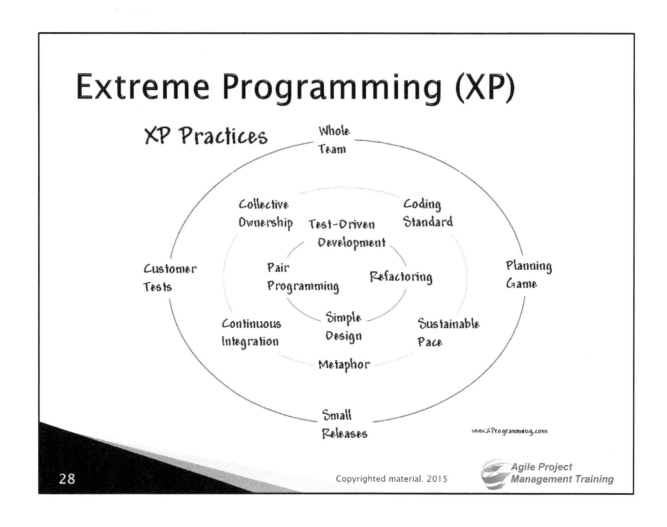

Copyrighted material. 2015

28

Agile Project Management Training

Notes:

| |
| |
| |
| |
| |
| |
| |
| |

Extreme Programming (XP)

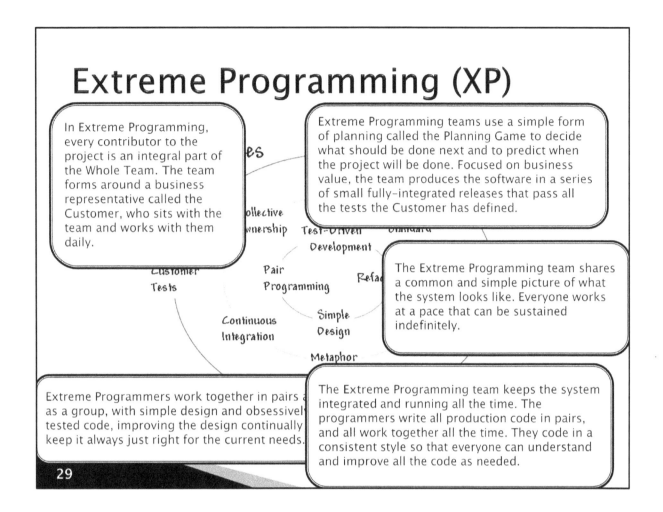

In Extreme Programming, every contributor to the project is an integral part of the Whole Team. The team forms around a business representative called the Customer, who sits with the team and works with them daily.

Extreme Programming teams use a simple form of planning called the Planning Game to decide what should be done next and to predict when the project will be done. Focused on business value, the team produces the software in a series of small fully-integrated releases that pass all the tests the Customer has defined.

The Extreme Programming team shares a common and simple picture of what the system looks like. Everyone works at a pace that can be sustained indefinitely.

Extreme Programmers work together in pairs and as a group, with simple design and obsessively tested code, improving the design continually to keep it always just right for the current needs.

The Extreme Programming team keeps the system integrated and running all the time. The programmers write all production code in pairs, and all work together all the time. They code in a consistent style so that everyone can understand and improve all the code as needed.

Collective Ownership

Customer Tests

Test-Driven Development

Pair Programming

Refactoring

Continuous Integration

Simple Design

Metaphor

29

Notes:

Page 29

Extreme Programming

Whole Team
- In Extreme Programming, every contributor to the project is an integral part of the "Whole Team". The team forms around a business representative called "the Customer", who sits with the team and works with them daily.

Planning Game, Small Releases, Customer Tests
- Extreme Programming teams use a simple form of planning and tracking to decide what should be done next and to predict when the project will be done. Focused on business value, the team produces the software in a series of small fully-integrated releases that pass all the tests the Customer has defined.

Simple Design, Pair Programming, Test-Driven Development, Design Improvement
- Extreme Programmers work together in pairs and as a group, with simple design and obsessively tested code, improving the design continually to keep it always just right for the current needs.

Continuous Integration, Collective Code Ownership, Coding Standards
- The Extreme Programming team keeps the system integrated and running all the time. The programmers write all production code in pairs, and all work together all the time. They code in a consistent style so that everyone can understand and improve all the code as needed.

Metaphor, Sustainable Pace
- The Extreme Programming team shares a common and simple picture of what the system looks like. Everyone works at a pace that can be sustained indefinitely.

30

Copyrighted material. 2015

 *Agile Project Management Training*

Notes:

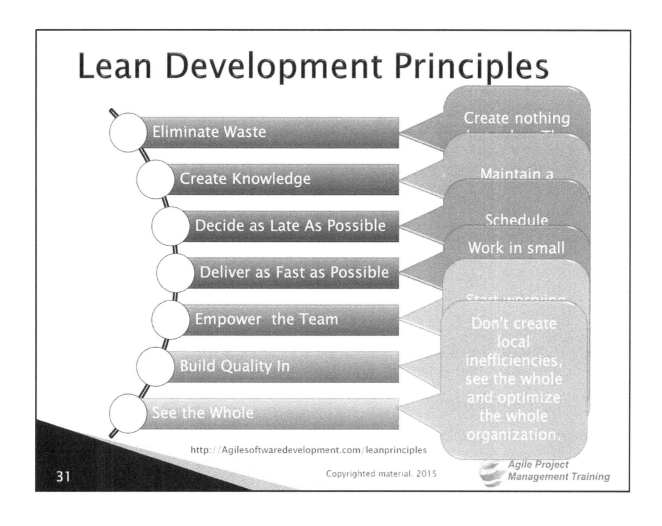

Lean Development Principles

1. **Eliminate Waste**
   - Create nothing but value. The less code you write, the less code you have to test.

2. **Create Knowledge**
   - Maintain a culture of constant learning and improvement.

3. **Decide as Late as Possible**
   - Schedule Irreversible Decisions at the Last Responsible Moment.

4. **Deliver as Fast as Possible**
   - Work in small batches – reduce projects size, shorten release cycles, stabilize work environment.

5. **Empower The Team**
   - Move responsibility and decision making to the lowest possible level.

6. **Build Quality In**
   - Start worrying about it before you write single line of working code.

7. **See the Whole**
   - Don't create local inefficiencies, see the whole and optimize the whole organization.

32

Copyrighted material. 2015

Agile Project Management Training

Notes:

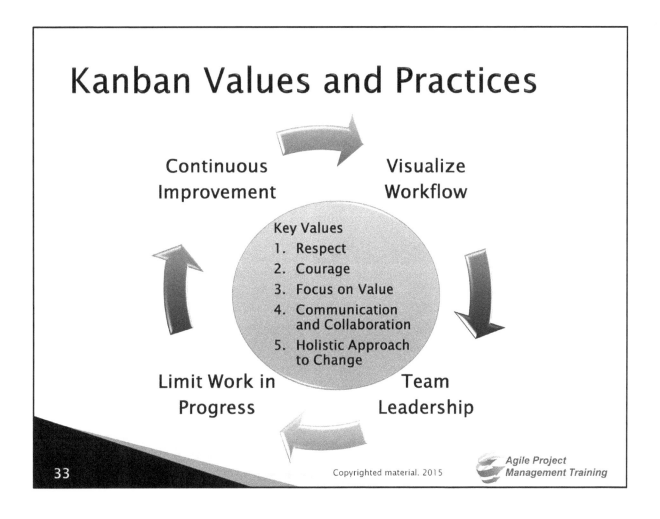

How it all Fits Together

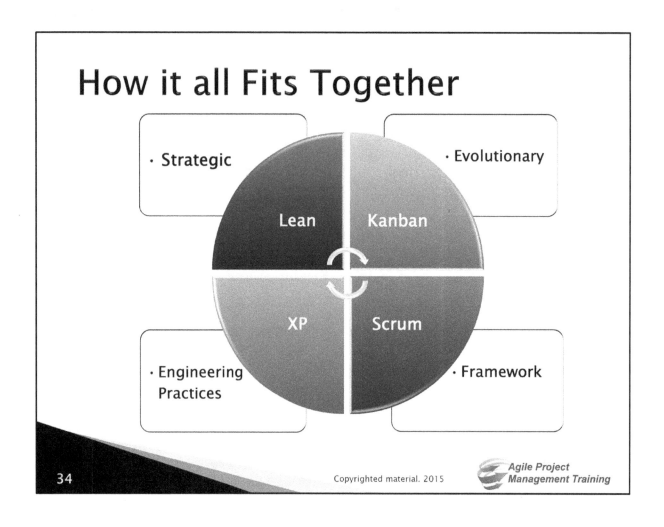

- Strategic
- Evolutionary
- Engineering Practices
- Framework

Lean

Kanban

XP

Scrum

Copyrighted material. 2015

Agile Project
Management Training

Notes:

Discussion

Which Agile approaches has your
organization tried?
What worked?
What didn't?

Copyrighted material. 2015

*Agile Project
Management Training*

Notes:

Simple Kanban

Copyrighted material. 2015

Agile Project
Management Training

Copyrighted material. 2015

Notes:

Kanban

- Developed by Taiichi Ohno when he saw the demand-based inventory management of grocery stores in the U.S. in the 1940s.
- Toyota originally used Kanban cards to limit the amount of inventory tied up in work in progress (WIP) on a manufacturing floor.
- Kanban is part of an overall Lean approach to eliminate waste in a system and focus production on high-value work.
- Using a Kanban approach in software drops time-boxed iterations in favor of focusing on continuous flow.
- Kanban for software development typically has little or no prescriptive "rules" and allows organizations to evolve from where they are today.

Copyrighted material. 2015

Agile Project Management Training

37

Notes:

5 Values of Kanban

1. Respect
2. Courage
3. Focus on Value
4. Communication and Collaboration
5. Holistic Approach to Change

38

Copyrighted material. 2015

Agile Project Management Training

Notes:

1. Respect

- At the core of Lean is respecting people. Respect for people also means assuming responsibility for your actions, and empowering others to take those actions.
- Respect for people allows for delegation and the demand-pull that is crucial to Kanban. When any developer is able to take a story from the backlog and pull it to development or QA, he is able to do so because we respect him, we respect his skills, and we give him the ability to do so.
- Respect for people also aligns with sustainable pace in Agile, or Muri in Lean.

39

Copyrighted material. 2015

Agile Project Management Training

Notes:

2. Courage

- Courage and respect are primary values in XP:
  - "If members of a team don't care about each other and their work, no methodology can work. You must be respectful to your colleagues and their contributions, to your organization, and to persons whose life is touched by the system you are writing."*
- In order to improve or even correct mistakes we need courage.
- Courage combined with respect for people enable effective delegation, proper demand-pull and continuous improvement.

* Kent Beck, with Cynthia Andres, "Extreme Programming Explained — Embrace Change", Second Edition, Addison Wesley 2005.

40

Copyrighted material. 2015

 *Agile Project Management Training*

Notes:

3. Focus on Value

▸ One of the key purposes of Kanban is the creation of value. In software development value means the creation of working, quality code. Value implies customer satisfaction, and that is ultimately the purpose of our efforts.

▸ Value is at the center of Lean and TPS, but frequently it is mentioned as the reverse side of the coin: eliminate waste or "Muda" in Japanese Muda represents anything that does not add value to your process or flow. By eliminating waste, we optimize the creation of value.

41

Copyrighted material. 2015

Agile Project
Management Training

Notes:

4. Communication and Collaboration

- Communication, and collaboration are at the center of teamwork. One value does not work without the other. To succeed we need to make ourselves heard but also we need to be able to work with others to create value.
- Without teamwork Kanban fails. Any business that does not communicate and collaborate properly will fail.

Copyrighted material. 2015

Agile Project Management Training

42

Notes:

5. Holistic Approach to Change

- We need to take a holistic view of the system and understand it.
- Deming's System of Profound Knowledge and Goldratt's Theory of Constraints states that no single part of a system can ever bring overall improvement.
- A key part of the system is people, not just as resources, but also as individuals who make the system work.
- Kanban aims to drive improvement where it counts. An understanding of the whole is fundamental to arrive at steady, successful change.

43

Copyrighted material. 2015

 *Agile Project Management Training*

Notes:

4 Key Practices of Kanban

1. Visualize the workflow.
2. Team Leadership
3. Limit Work in Progress (WIP)
4. Continuous Improvement

44   Copyrighted material. 2015    *Agile Project Management Training*

Notes:

1. Visualize the workflow

- When we are doing knowledge work most of the work is invisible.
  - It is easy to see the final product of knowledge work: a website, a book, a report; but it is hard to see progress of the work.
- Use Kanban boards for visual representations of workflow.
- Advantages of Kanban boards:
  - You can look at the system, not just the flow
  - Ability to map the value chain
  - Easy live collaboration
  - Near real-time status of the project

Copyrighted material. 2015

Agile Project
Management Training

45

Kanban Board

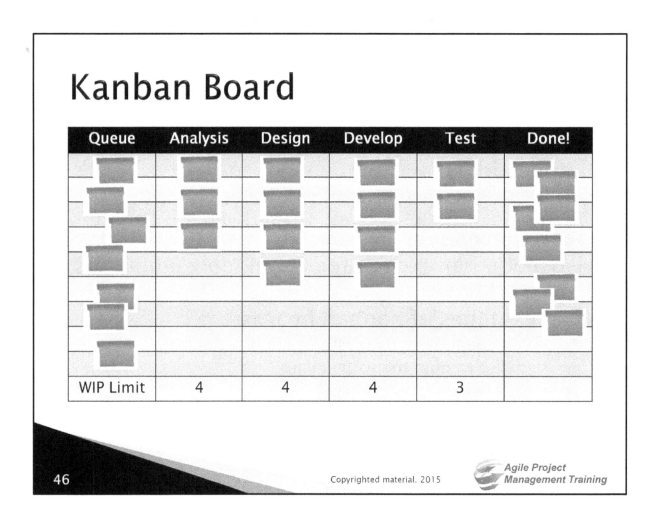

Queue	Analysis	Design	Develop	Test	Done!
WIP Limit	4	4	4	3	

Copyrighted material. 2015

Agile Project Management Training

Notes:

2. Team Leadership

- Unlike Scrum, Kanban does not require you to create new roles or change your organization.
- Through team leadership you manage flow and benefit the whole team and the organization.
- Commit to continuously learn and improve the way you manage teams.

Copyrighted material. 2015

 *Agile Project Management Training*

Notes:

3. Limit Work in Progress (WIP)

▸ WIP is the amount of work you attempt to do at any given time. It can apply to:

  ◦ The amount of To-Dos you have on your day
  ◦ The number of stories (distinct software features) you are developing right now
  ◦ The size of those stories, the larger they are the harder it will be to deliver them
  ◦ The amount of multitasking you do

Copyrighted material. 2015

Agile Project Management Training

Notes:

Benefits of Limiting WIP

- By reducing WIP, you accelerate delivery, this allows for faster feedback and therefore less risk.
- Reducing WIP leads to faster cycle times = faster time to market.
- It focuses the people and the team allowing them to multitask less and deliver more value.

49

Copyrighted material. 2015

Agile Project Management Training

Notes:

4. Continuous Improvement

- ▸ The 3 previous practices are intended to do things better than before.
- ▸ Significant improvements to innovation, morale, culture and productivity require that we stop, learn and apply our knowledge to improve.
- ▸ Learning is the key concept before continuous improvement can ever happen. Adopt it in your team, and in your company culture.

50

Copyrighted material. 2015

 Agile Project Management Training

Notes:

Continuous Improvement in Kanban

- Have effective Kanban Meetings
  - Stand-ups
  - Demos
  - Release Planning
- Hold Retrospectives
- Manage product backlog collaboratively across the organization
- Train your team
- Encourage a culture that welcomes risk and innovation

51

Copyrighted material. 2015

 *Agile Project Management Training*

Notes:

Your First Kanban Project

1. Define a work process flow
2. Lay out a Kanban board
3. Decide on limits for items in queue and work in progress
4. Document release goal
5. Place prioritized stories or features in queue
6. Move features through the process flow as work is completed
7. Calculate Cycle Time

http://www.agileproductdesign.com/downloads/patton_kanban.ppt

Copyrighted material. 2015

52

Notes:

1. Define a Work Process Flow

▸ Look at the typical flow for features, stories, or work packages and describe typical process steps.

- Analysis
- Design
- Develop
- Test

Copyrighted material. 2015

Agile Project Management Training

Notes:

2. Lay Out a Kanban Board

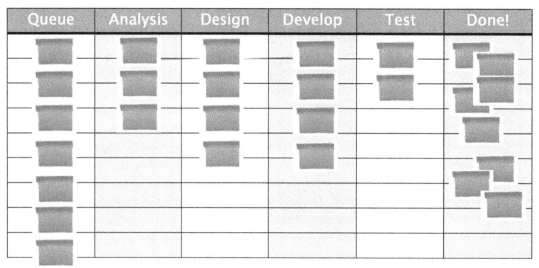

> ‣ Create columns with a work queue on the left, the process steps in the middle, and a final "done" column to the right.

Copyrighted material. 2015

Agile Project Management Training

Notes:

Page 54

3. Decide on Limits for Items in Queue & WIP

- ‣ WIP is initially a guess
- ‣ Adjust the WIP based upon flow
- ‣ Work backs up = Lower WIP
- ‣ Team members have idle time = Increase WIP
- ‣ Trial and error

Copyrighted material. 2015

Agile Project Management Training

Notes:

3. Decide on Limits for Items in Queue & WIP (cont'd)

Queue	Analysis	Design	Develop	Test	Done!
WIP	**20 hours**	**40 hours**	**80 hours**	**20 hours**	

▸ The WIP limit can be in number of items, story points or hours. Put the WIP limit on the bottom of each column

Copyrighted material. 2015

Agile Project Management Training

Notes:

4. Document Release Goal

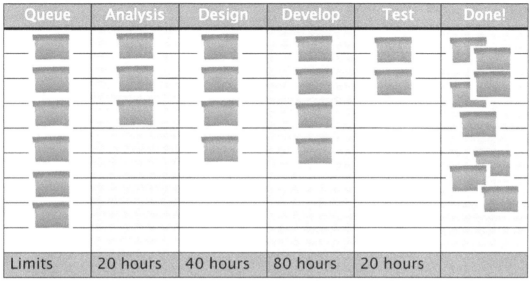

Queue	Analysis	Design	Develop	Test	Done!
Limits	20 hours	40 hours	80 hours	20 hours	

Goal: New Web Interface

> ‣ A good goal describes the outcome we hope to achieve. Goals help keep a focus on the larger outcome.

Copyrighted material. 2015

57

Agile Project Management Training

Notes:

5. Start the Board by Placing Stories or Features in Queue

Queue	Analysis	Design	Develop	Test	Done!
6/1					
6/1					
6/2					
6/3					
6/3					
6/4					
Limits	20 hours	40 hours	80 hours	20 hours	

> ‣ Mark on the story or feature card the date it entered the queue. This is the start date. This begins our measurement of cycle time.

Copyrighted material. 2015

Agile Project Management Training

Notes:

6. Move Features through the Process Flow as Work is Completed

Queue	Analysis	Design	Develop	Test	Done!
					2d
					2d
					3d
					1.5d
					4d
Limits	20 hours	40 hours	80 hours	20 hours	

As it's finished, write the number of days it took to complete, that is the cycle time for that item.

Copyrighted material. 2015

Agile Project Management Training

59

Notes:

7. Use the Dates on the Cards to Calculate Cycle Time

Queue	Analysis	Design	Develop	Test	Done!
Limits	20 hours	40 hours	80 hours	20 hours	

› Capture the average cycle time daily for all items that are done. Use a 3 month rolling average to set wait times, SLAs and perform resource planning. Pay attention to flow and bottlenecks; relieving bottlenecks as quickly as possible.

Copyrighted material. 2015

Agile Project Management Training

60

Notes:

Kanban Management

- Keep regular time-boxes for product inspection
- Evaluate the quality of the growing product from a functional, engineering, and user experience perspective
- Evaluate the pace of development:
  - Look at the number of development items completed relative to goals
  - Look at the average cycle time per development item
  - Adjust the development plan as necessary
  - Evaluate and adjust the process being used
  - Use retrospectives to identify changes to improve your product or pace

61

Copyrighted material. 2015

*Agile Project
Management Training*

Notes:

| |
| |
| |
| |
| |
| |
| |
| |

Kanban + Scrum + XP= Success

Copyrighted material. 2015

Agile Project
Management Training

62

Notes:

Scrum

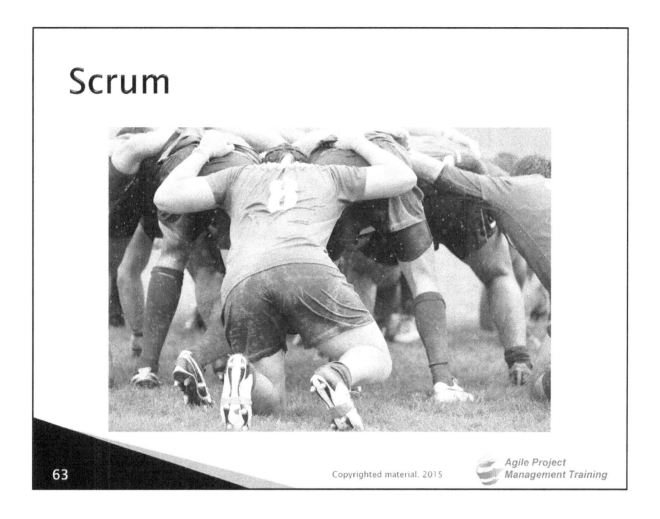

Copyrighted material. 2015

Agile Project Management Training

63

Notes:

Scrum is:

- Scrum is a lightweight, simple to understand (but difficult to master) agile process framework.
- Scrum is one of many agile software development methods.
- Scrum and Extreme Programming (XP) are probably the two best-known Agile methods. XP emphasizes technical practices such as pair programming and continuous integration. Scrum emphasizes management practices such as the role of Scrum Master.
- Many companies use the management practices of Scrum with the engineering practices of XP.

64

Copyrighted material. 2015

Agile Project Management Training

Notes:

Key Characteristics of Scrum

- ▸ Relies on self–organizing teams
- ▸ The product progresses in a series of month–long (or shorter) "Sprints"
- ▸ Requirements are captured in a list called a "product backlog"
- ▸ No specific engineering practices are prescribed
- ▸ Relies on the empirical process of trial and error to continuously improve

65

Copyrighted material. 2015

Agile Project Management Training

Notes:

Scrum & Kanban differences

Scrum	Kanban Approach
Fixed Iterations/Sprints	Continuous delivery
Cross functional team	Work with existing team model
Sprint Planning occurs one per Sprint	Ongoing backlog management
Sprint Backlogs are frozen and completed every Sprint	Kanban board is never "done"
No change during Sprint	Change is frequent, only limiter is WIP
Burndown Charts are sued to track progress	Cumulative flow diagrams are used
Sprint velocity is the measurement of capacity and throughput	Cycle time is the key measurement

Copyrighted material. 2015

Agile Project Management Training

Notes:

Benefits of Kanban over Scrum

- Using a Kanban approach to software development eliminates time-boxed iterations in favor of focusing on continuous flow.
- Common problems in Scrum include:
  - Short time-boxes give more frequent opportunity to measure progress and inspect software but force development items to be smaller
  - Smaller development items are often too small to be valuable and difficult to identify
  - Quality of requirements suffers as analysts rush to prepare for upcoming cycles
  - Quality of current development suffers when busy analysts are unable to inspect software or answer questions during development
  - Quality often suffers as the team races to complete work late in the development time-box

67

Copyrighted material. 2015

 *Agile Project Management Training*

Notes:

| |
| |
| |
| |
| |
| |
| |

Scrum "Keepers"

The Scrum framework has created prescriptive roles, meetings and artifacts that may have value to a Kanban approach:

- Scrum Roles
  - Product Owner
  - Scrum Master attributes in a Kanban Lead
  - Small self-organized Team
- Scrum Meetings
  - Daily Scrum/Stand-up
  - Retrospectives
  - Backlog Planning/Grooming
  - Demos (Sprint Reviews)
- Scrum Artifacts
  - Product Backlog
- Definition of "Done"

Copyrighted material. 2015

Agile Project Management Training

68

Notes:

XP Engineering Best Practices for Kanban

As with Scrum, Kanban does not prescribe engineering practices. The following XP practices should be considered to create a high-performing software development team:

- Simple Design
- Pair Programming
- Test-Driven Development
- Continuous Integration
- Collective Code Ownership
- Coding Standards

69

Copyrighted material. 2015

Agile Project Management Training

Notes:

The Kanban Team

Copyrighted material. 2015

70

Agile Project
Management Training

Notes:

The Kanban Team

▸ Kanban doesn't prescribe specific roles.
▸ High-performing Kanban teams function with the following roles:
  ◦ Kanban Lead
  ◦ Product Manager/Product Owner
  ◦ Team Members

Copyrighted material. 2015

Agile Project
Management Training

Notes:

The Kanban Lead

- Similar to the role of a Scrum Master
- Represents management to the project
- Responsible for promoting the 5 Kanban Values
- Helps team members remove impediments
- Ensures that the team is fully functional and productive
- Shields the team from external interferences
- Can be a member of the Team
- Is a Servant Leader

72

Copyrighted material. 2015

Agile Project Management Training

Notes:

A Servant Leader

- ‣ Facilitates the team to address the tasks
- ‣ Fosters an environment that is trusting and respectful; supports collaboration
- ‣ Critical to building self–organizing teams
- ‣ A more challenging role, but more rewarding

73

Copyrighted material. 2015

Agile Project
Management Training

Notes:

| |
| |
| |
| |
| |
| |
| |
| |

Servant Leader Success Criteria

- ‣ Make sure you have the right people on the team:
  - ◦ Passion
  - ◦ Skills
  - ◦ Capacity
- ‣ Trust first
- ‣ Let the team members propose the approach to make the project a success
- ‣ Provide support, remove obstacles and stay out of the way

74

Copyrighted material. 2015

Agile Project Management Training

Notes:

Being an Effective Servant Leader

- Learn the team members' needs.
- Learn the project's requirements.
- Act for the simultaneous welfare of the team and the project.
- Create an environment of functional accountability.
- Serve as the central figure in successful project team development.

75

Copyrighted material. 2015

Agile Project Management Training

Notes:

An Agile Leadership Model

Components

- Process Knowledge
- Technical Skillset
- Business Experience
- Facilitation Skills
- Training Skills
- Coaching Skills

Levels

- Beginner
- Practitioner
- Master
- Coach
- Expert

76

Copyrighted material. 2015

Agile Project
Management Training

Copyrighted material. 2015

Notes:

Activity

Agile Leadership
Self–Assessment

Copyrighted material. 2015

77

Notes:

Activity: Agile Self-Assessment

Directions:

1. Review and identify your level for each component of the matrix.
2. What is your highest competency?
3. What competency do you need to work on most?
4. What competency are you strong at but don't really enjoy?
5. Pair-up and review

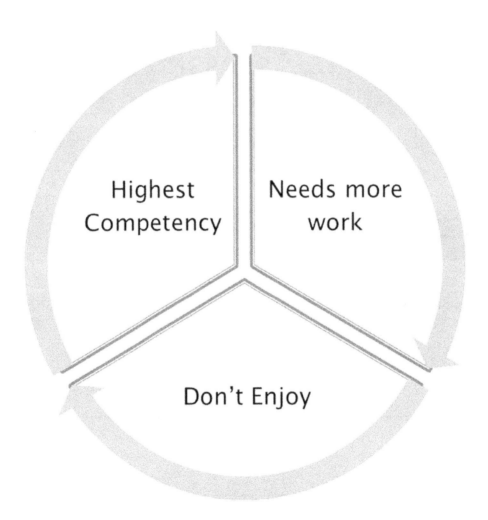

	Beginner	Practitioner	Master	Coach	Expert
Process Knowledge	Aware of principles and practices. Participated in an Agile project	Understand the principles and practices. Actively working in and improving an Agile project	Can setup and lead an Agile project. Experience as an iteration Manager/ Scrum Master	Significant Agile project experience in varied environments. Can adapt to suit project environments	Well recognized with the industry and maintain public presence.
Technical Skillset	Work in a team using core skills (BA, Dev, Tester, PM)	Lead of a discipline within a team. Established standard of practice and quality within a team	Remains current with best practice and industry trends in relevant discipline.	Recognized by peers as a technical expert in relevant discipline.	Creating and publishing new techniques.
Business Experience	Clear understanding of the business, the operating environment and the market	Comfortable discussing business process. Understand factors influencing business success.	Understand market trends and strategy. Sought after for business advice and analysis of impacts.	Understand risk, finance and strategic elements that impact business. Experience running a business unit.	Have run a successful business in your industry. Sought after to advise on running business.
Facilitation Skills	Comfortable working with and leading a group. Ad-hoc facilitation of Agile team ceremonies.	Experienced in facilitating group discussion of complex issues. Leads the facilitation of Agile team ceremonies.	Leads multi-day workshops and planning events for large or newly formed teams.	Facilitates sessions involving complex people issues. Facilitates sessions involving multiple stakeholders and conflicting priorities.	Facilitates senior executive sessions and/or large groups of people.
Training Skills	Enjoy helping other learn. Supports learning initiatives within the team environment.	Have some experience delivering training to small teams.	Comfortable delivering training to larger groups. Participate in developing and updating training content.	Significant training experience across multiple courses. Comfortable writing and piloting new course content.	Recognized and sought after as a trainer. Have trained a number of other trainers.
Coaching Skills	Understand the role and difference between coach, mentor and advisor.	Can provide ad-hoc coaching within current team.	Recognized as a leader and am able to follow a simple coaching model for helping people to resolve their own problems.	Adapt coaching style to suit situation, team and staff level. Comfortable coaching peers and executive staff.	Recognized and sought after as a coach not only in Agile but in other areas of work. Capable of coaching C-level executives

The Product Owner

- Same role and title as in Scrum
- Defines the features of the product
- Decides on the release date and content
- Is responsible for the profitability of the product (ROI)
- Prioritizes features according to market value
- Adjusts features and priority as needed

Copyrighted material. 2015

Notes:

The Kanban Team

- The Scrum prescription of 6+/- 3 people is a good guideline for team size. Smaller teams are more productive.
- Differences with between Scrum and Kanban is that the people working on different parts of the process don't need to work together all the time.
- The team size should be kept manageable for those members of the team who need to communicate and co-ordinate with each other regularly
- Typically, the team members are initially specialists: Programmers, testers, user experience designers, etc., and over time they will become more cross-functional as they jump in to help with blockages.

82

Copyrighted material. 2015

Agile Project
Management Training

Notes:

Self-organizing Team Challenges

- "Pull" processes such used in Scrum, XP and Kanban require a motivated, high-performing team
- For many organizational cultures, it is the most unique component of Agile
- Often the biggest and most difficult change
- Existing personnel problems are often highlighted or exacerbated

Copyrighted material. 2015

Agile Project Management Training

Notes:

Empowering a self-organizing team

- Leadership needs to set the common goal and shared vision
- Establish a knowledge-sharing environment that includes trust, openness and feedback loops.
- Give each member some authority (might create conflicts).
- Let the team decide!

84

Copyrighted material. 2015

 Agile Project Management Training

Notes:

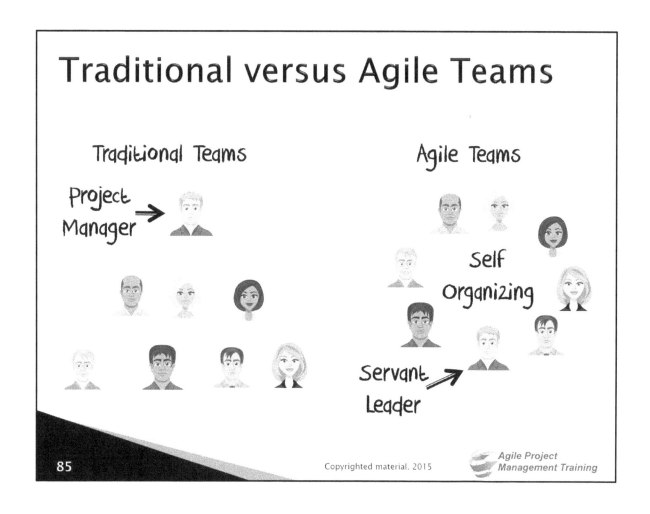

Traditional versus Agile Teams

Traditional Teams

Project Manager →

Agile Teams

Self Organizing

Servant Leader →

Copyrighted material. 2015

85

Agile Project Management Training

Notes:

Discussion

Have you ever been on a high-performing team?

What were some of the attributes?

Copyrighted material. 2015

86

Agile Project
Management Training

Notes:

Benefits of a Self-organizing Team

- Promotes creativity and problem solving throughout the organization
- Speeds adaptation to change
- Generates high-quality products and services
- Decreases the odds of burnout
- Supports leadership among peers

87

Copyrighted material. 2015

 *Agile Project Management Training*

Notes:

Kanban Team Success Criteria

1. Self–organizing team members have to be more creative
2. Have to have a strong discipline and work ethic
3. Must be committed to the project's goals
4. Respect each other
5. Share a genuine conviction that the "we"—the potent concept behind every team—will succeed or fail together

Copyrighted material. 2015

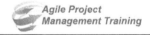

Agile Project Management Training

Notes:

How Teams Develop

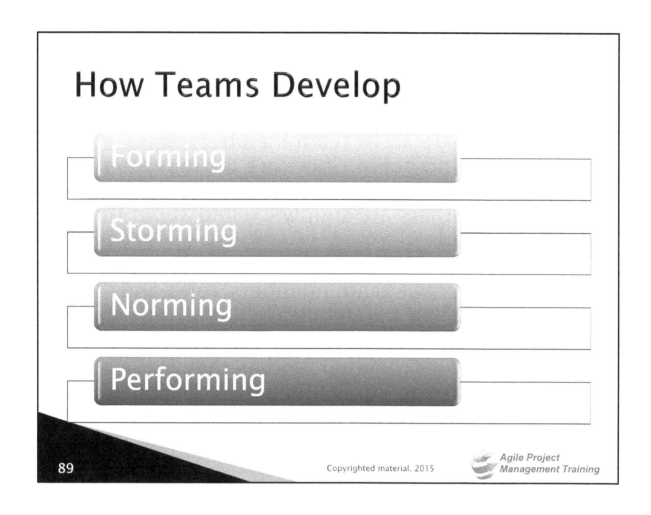

Copyrighted material. 2015

Agile Project
Management Training

89

Notes:

Forming

- In this stage, most team members are positive and polite. Some are anxious, as they haven't fully understood what work the team will do. Others are simply excited about the task ahead.
- The leader will play a dominant role at this stage, because team members' roles and responsibilities aren't clear.
- This stage can last for some time, as people start to work together, and as they make an effort to get to know their new colleagues.

Copyrighted material. 2015

90

Notes:

Storming

- This is the stage where many teams fail.
- Storming often starts where there is a conflict between team members' natural working styles.
- If it has not been clearly defined how the team will work, people may feel overwhelmed by their workload.
- Some people may question the worth of the team's goal, and they may resist taking on tasks.
- Team members who stick with the task at hand may experience stress, particularly as they don't have the support of established processes, or strong relationships with their colleagues.

Copyrighted material. 2015

 *Agile Project Management Training*

Notes:

Norming

- This is when people start to resolve their differences, appreciate colleagues' strengths, and respect the leader.
- Now that the team members know one another better, they may socialize together, and they are able to ask each other for help and provide constructive feedback.
- People develop a stronger commitment to the team goal, and start to see good progress towards it.
- There is often a prolonged overlap between storming and norming, because, as new tasks come up, the team may lapse back into behavior from the storming stage.

92

Copyrighted material. 2015

 Agile Project
Management Training

Notes:

Performing

- The team reaches the performing stage when hard work and minimal friction leads to the achievement of the team's goal.
- The structures and processes set up support this well.
- The leader can concentrate on developing individual team members.
- It feels easy to be part of the team at this stage, and people who join or leave won't disrupt performance.

93

Copyrighted material. 2015

 *Agile Project Management Training*

Notes:

Team Communication in Agile

- ‣ Face-to-face
- ‣ Osmotic communication
- ‣ Distributed teams

94

Copyrighted material. 2015

Agile Project Management Training

Notes:

Face-to-Face Communication

- ▸ "The most efficient and effective method of conveying information to and within a development team is face-to-face conversation." – the Agile Manifesto
- ▸ Co-located teams benefits from this type of communication
- ▸ User story creation with team members present is highly desirable
- ▸ Providing feedback would be desirable face-to face

95

Copyrighted material. 2015

 Agile Project Management Training

Notes:

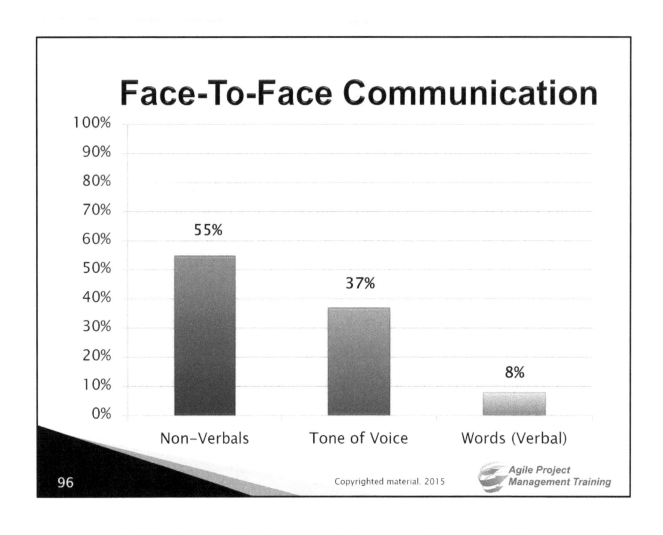

Copyrighted material. 2015

Agile Project Management Training

Notes:

Osmotic Communication

- The basis of the open workspace model
- Information flows into the background hearing of team members
- Pick up relevant information as though by osmosis
- Supports fewer meetings
- Studies show double the productivity and decreased time to market

Copyrighted material. 2015

Agile Project
Management Training

97

Notes:

Open Workspace Design Example

Rolling whiteboards

http://jamesshore.com/Agile-Book/sit_together.html

Copyrighted material. 2015

Agile Project
Management Training

98

Notes:

Distributed Teams

Distributed teams have more challenges. To overcome these challenges:

- Leverage technology
  - Email
  - SMS/instant messaging
  - Video conferencing
  - Interactive white boards
  - Collaboration tools
- Commit to more informal communications
  - Unplanned calls
  - Acknowledge personal topics; birthdays, etc.

Copyrighted material. 2015

Agile Project Management Training

Notes:

Activity

Who does what on a Kanban project?

Copyrighted material. 2015

Agile Project Management Training

Notes:

Exercise: Who does what?

	Team	Product Owner	Kanban Lead
Provides Estimates			
Prioritizes Backlog			
Creates User Stories			
Performs User Acceptance			
Facilitates Meetings			
Promotes Kanban Values			
Pulls Tasks			
Makes Technical Decisions			
Designs Software			
Removes Impediments			
Defines Done			
Assign Tasks			

Exercise: Who does what?

	Team	Product Owner	Kanban Lead
Provides Estimates	x		
Prioritizes Backlog		x	
Creates User Stories		x	
Performs User Acceptance		x	
Facilitates Meetings			x
Promotes Kanban Values			x
Pulls Tasks	x		
Makes Technical Decisions	x		
Designs Software	x		
Removes Impediments	x	x	x
Defines Done	x	x	
Assign Tasks		no one	

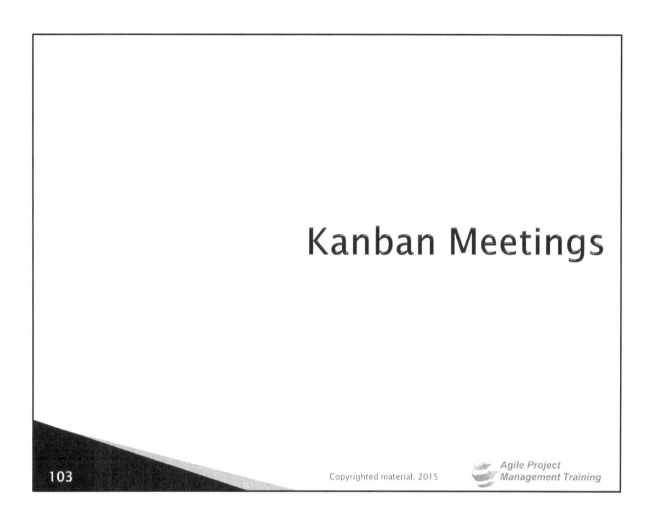

Kanban Meetings

Copyrighted material. 2015

Agile Project
Management Training

103

Kanban Meetings

- Kanban does not prescribe any particular meetings but best-practices include:
  - Daily Standups
  - Backlog Grooming
  - Release Planning
  - Retrospectives
  - Demos
- Best practice reccomendation: no more than 10% of time spent in meetings.

Copyrighted material. 2015

Agile Project
Management Training

Notes:

The Daily Standup

- ▸ Similar to Daily Scrum
  - ◦ Daily
  - ◦ Same time
  - ◦ 15–minutes
  - ◦ Stand–up
- ▸ Only conversation is to provide an update on their Kanban task
- ▸ Not for problem solving
- ▸ Only the team needs to attend
- ▸ Helps avoid other unnecessary meetings

105

Copyrighted material. 2015

Agile Project Management Training

Notes:

Backlog Grooming

- Unique to Agile
- Constant review and prioritization of the Backlog
- Product Owner and Kanban Team
- Focus is on clarifying product backlog items
- Typically help once a week for one to two hours.

Copyrighted material. 2015

 Agile Project
Management Training

Notes:

Release Planning

- ‣ Product owner presents a release goal and selects those items from the product backlog she thinks will meet the goal
- ‣ Occurs based upon the product release schedule – once per release cycle, though no more than once per week.
- ‣ Include the product owner and team
- ‣ The focus is on collaborative prioritization

Copyrighted material. 2015

Agile Project Management Training

107

Notes:

Product Demos

- Held prior to each release
- The Scrum approach should be considered:
  - Minimal prep and lightweight demos
  - Work is presented by the individual who built it
  - Only completed "done" items are demonstrated
  - Primary audience are stakeholders
  - Feedback is encouraged

Copyrighted material. 2015

Agile Project
Management Training

108

Notes:

Retrospectives

- Periodically take a look at what is and is not working in the process, technology, tools, etc.
- Typically performed every two-weeks
- Use a neutral facilitator
- Important to have open feedback
- Incorporate feedback immediately

Copyrighted material. 2015

Agile Project Management Training

Notes:

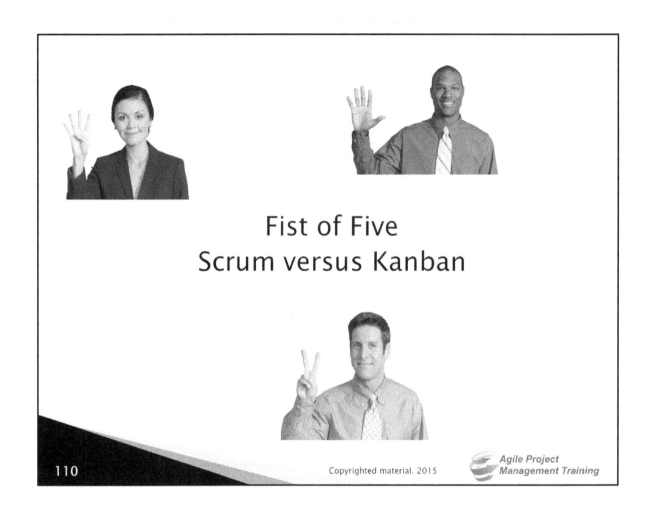

Fist of Five
Scrum versus Kanban

Copyrighted material. 2015

110

Agile Project
Management Training

Notes:

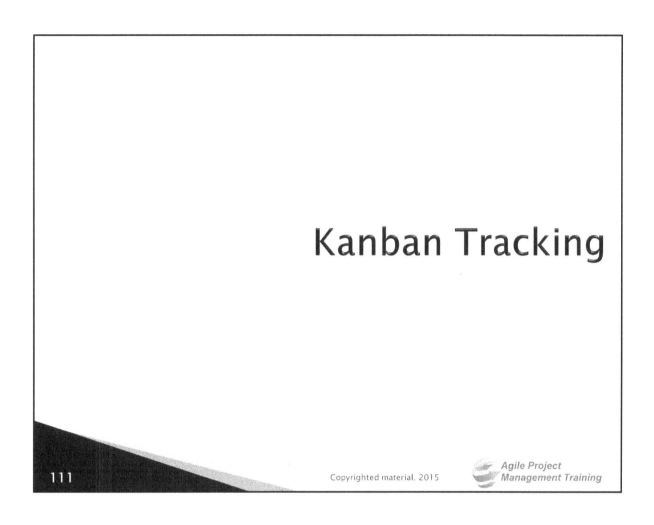

Kanban Tracking

Copyrighted material, 2015

Agile Project
Management Training

111

Notes:

Product Backlog

- A list high-level product requirements called "product backlog items" (PBIs)
- Common to most Agile approaches
- Ideally expressed such that each item has value to the users or customers of the product
- Prioritized by the product owner
- Reprioritized weekly
- Listed in the first column on the Kanban board

112

Copyrighted material. 2015

Agile Project
Management Training

Notes:

| |
| |
| |
| |
| |
| |
| |
| |

Kanban Board Options

- Columns can be general or very specific
- Items/tickets can be colored by type:
  - Feature
  - Enhancement
  - Defect
- Blockers can have a red ticket on top of them
- Swim lanes can be created by project, product, feature, epic, etc.
- Ultimately, let the team decide and evolve the board over time

113

Copyrighted material. 2015

Agile Project
Management Training

Notes:

A Simple Kanban Board

Product Requirements (Backlog)	In Progress	Completed (Done)
User Story User Story User Story User Story User Story User Story User Story	User Story User Story User Story	User Story User Story User Story User Story User Story User Story User Story

Copyrighted material. 2015

Agile Project Management Training

Notes:

Kanban Board Example

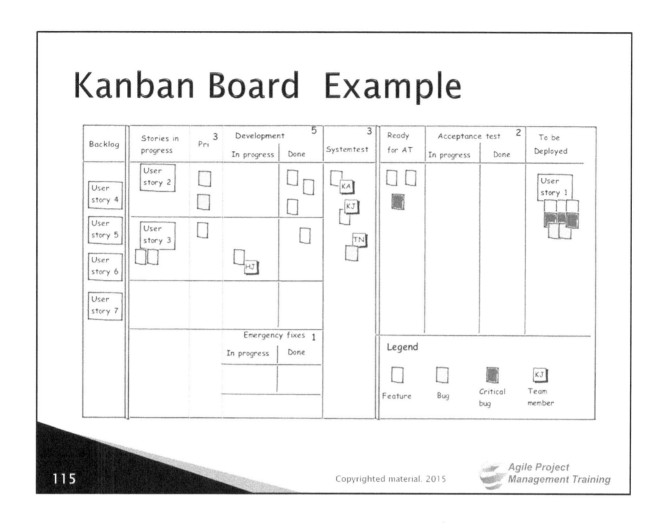

Copyrighted material. 2015

Agile Project
Management Training

Notes:

Kanban Board Example

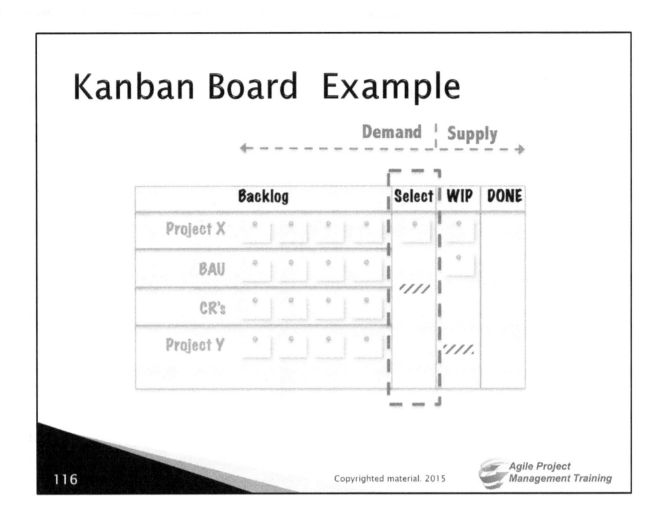

Copyrighted material. 2015

Agile Project Management Training

Notes:

Kanban Board Example

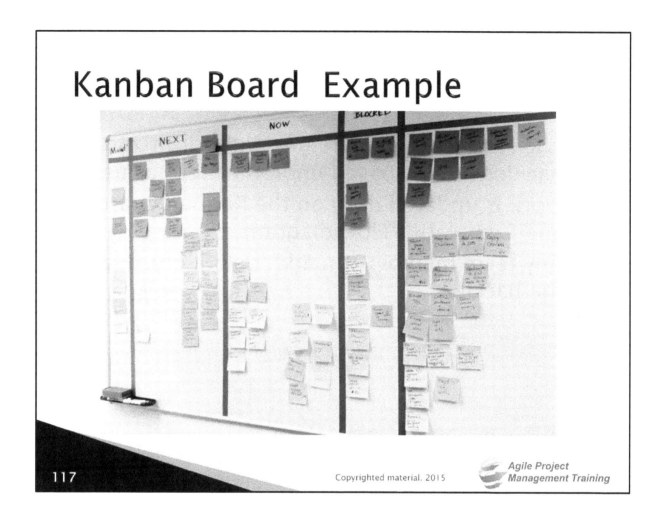

Copyrighted material. 2015

Agile Project Management Training

Notes:

Managing the backlog

- The Product Owner creates and prioritizes backlogs items based upon business value
- Work is updated daily on the Kanban board and Cumulative Flow diagram
- Any team member can add, delete or update the backlog

118

Copyrighted material. 2015

Agile Project Management Training

Notes:

Cumulative Flow Diagrams

- › Is an "information radiator" providing a visual display of development progress over time
- › Shows the different states that are defined in the Kanban board columns
- › Tracks the completion progress either by number of items, story points, hours ,etc.
- › Can show cycle time

119

Copyrighted material. 2015

Agile Project
Management Training

Notes:

Cumulative Flow Diagram Example

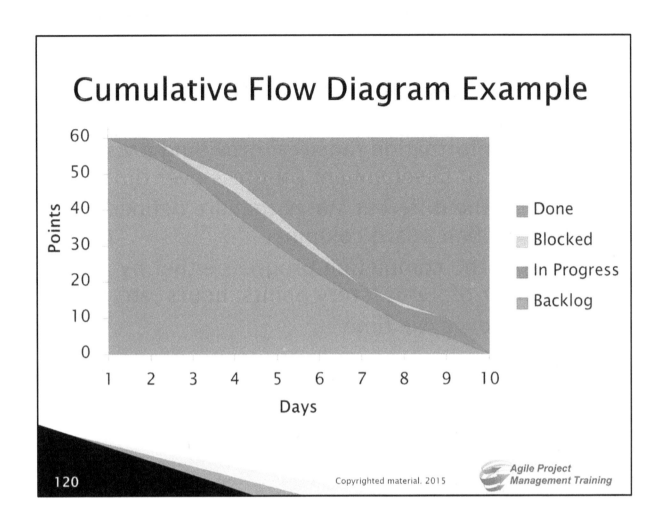

Copyrighted material. 2015

Agile Project
Management Training

Notes:

Cumulative Flow Diagram Example

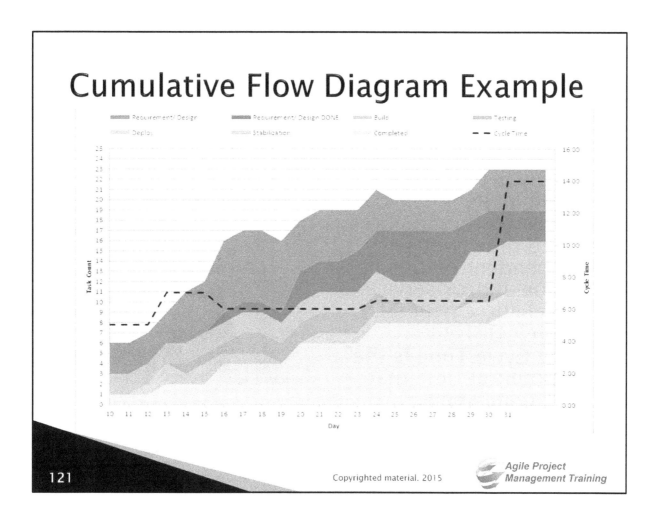

Copyrighted material. 2015

Agile Project Management Training

121

Notes:

Lead Time & Cycle Time

- The Lead time is the time from when and items is requested until an item is delivered.

- Lead time is often dependent on business value and/or service level agreement (SLA) with a customer.
- The Cycle Time is the amount of time that the team spent working on the item.

122

Copyrighted material. 2015

Agile Project
Management Training

Notes:

Using Cycle time for Release Planning

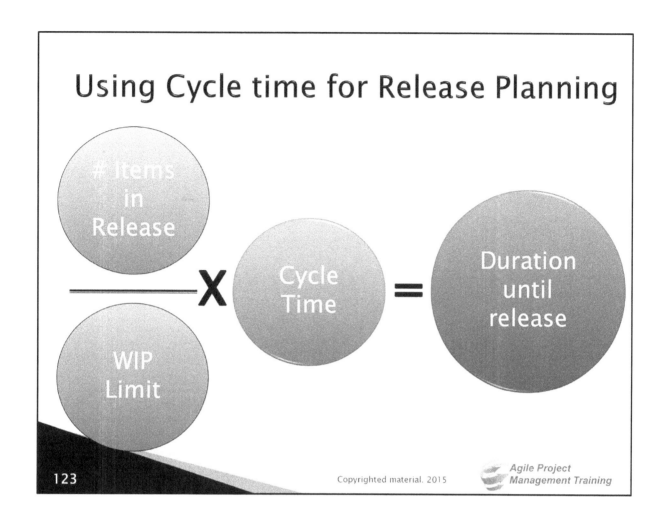

Copyrighted material. 2015

Agile Project Management Training

Notes:

Discussion

What can impact cycle time?

Copyrighted material. 2015

Agile Project
Management Training

Notes:

Kanban Software and Tools

- Critical for a dispersed team
- Support collaboration
- Used to track product backlog, tasks, progress, defects, issues
- Examples:
  - LeanKit, Trello, Rally, VersionOne, Jira
- An Agile tool does not make you Agile
- Remember, don't let the tool drive the project: "Individuals and Interactions over Processes and Tools"

125

Copyrighted material. 2015

Agile Project Management Training

Notes:

Activity

Day 1 Agile Review Game
http://bit.ly/AgileGames

Copyrighted material. 2015

126

Agile Project Management Training

Notes:

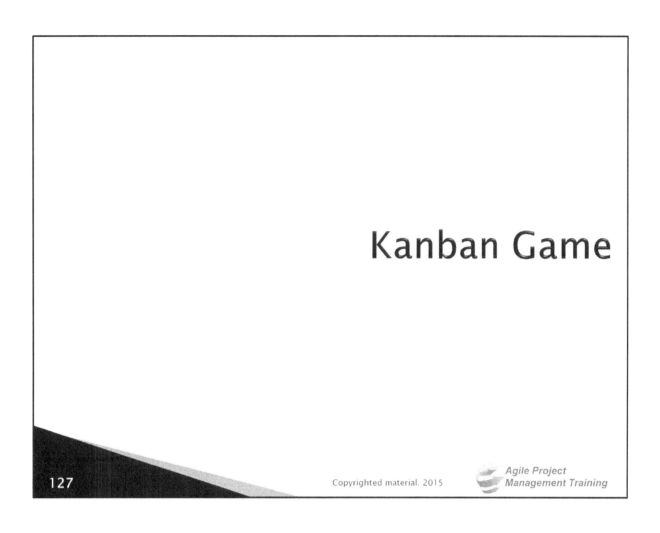

Kanban Game

Copyrighted material. 2015

Agile Project
Management Training

127

Notes:

The Goal

- Use an Agile/Kanban game to simulate running a project using Kanban
- Apply the principles we have learned
- Have Fun!

Copyrighted material. 2015

Agile Project Management Training

Notes:

Kanban Game Options

- The Kanban Pizza Game:
  - http://www.agile42.com/en/training/kanban-pizza-game/
  - http://www.slideshare.net/ralfhh/kanban-pizzagame
- Lego Kanban Game
  - http://www.leansimulations.org/2012/03/kanban-game-at-lego-pub.html
- Kanban Dice Game
  - http://www.leansimulations.org/2011/04/kanban-game-roll-snake-eyes-to-win.html
- and more...
  - http://www.leansimulations.org/p/huge-list-of-free-lean-games.html

129

Copyrighted material. 2015

 Agile Project Management Training

Notes:

| |
| |
| |
| |
| |
| |
| |
| |

Retrospective

▸ What did you learn?
▸ What would you do differently?

Copyrighted material. 2015

Agile Project
Management Training

130

Agile Product Lifecycle

131

Copyrighted material. 2015

Agile Project
Management Training

Notes:

Copyrighted material. 2015

Agile Project
Management Training

132

Notes:

Agile Planning Techniques

- Agile Roadmaps and Release Planning
- Users Stories for product backlog items
- Story points for WIP limits
- Relative Estimating

133

Copyrighted material. 2015

Agile Project
Management Training

Notes:

Agile Planning Frequency in Kanban

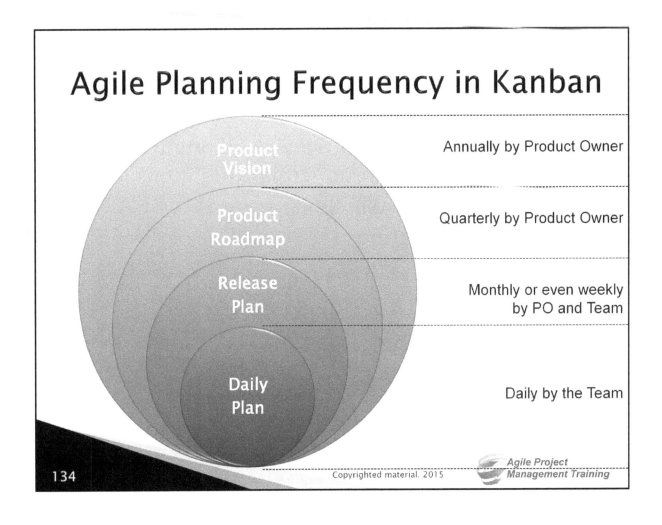

Product Vision — Annually by Product Owner

Product Roadmap — Quarterly by Product Owner

Release Plan — Monthly or even weekly by PO and Team

Daily Plan — Daily by the Team

Copyrighted material. 2015

Agile Project Management Training

134

Notes:

Agile Planning Approach

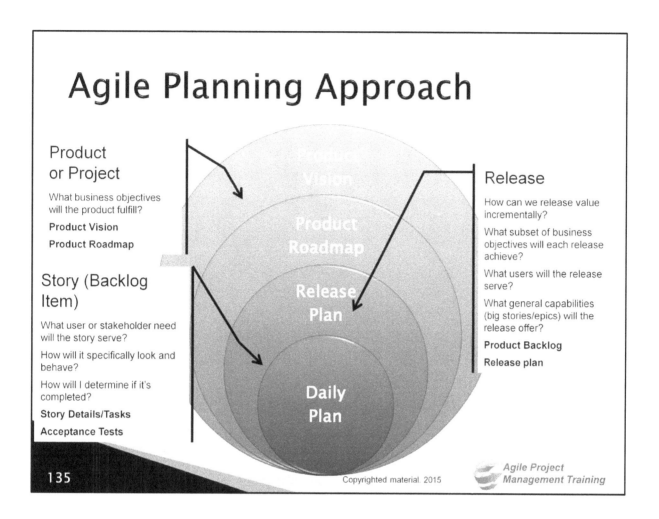

Product or Project

What business objectives will the product fulfill?

Product Vision

Product Roadmap

Story (Backlog Item)

What user or stakeholder need will the story serve?

How will it specifically look and behave?

How will I determine if it's completed?

Story Details/Tasks

Acceptance Tests

Product Vision

Product Roadmap

Release Plan

Daily Plan

Release

How can we release value incrementally?

What subset of business objectives will each release achieve?

What users will the release serve?

What general capabilities (big stories/epics) will the release offer?

Product Backlog

Release plan

135

Copyrighted material. 2015

Agile Project Management Training

Notes:

Agile Artifact Hierarchy

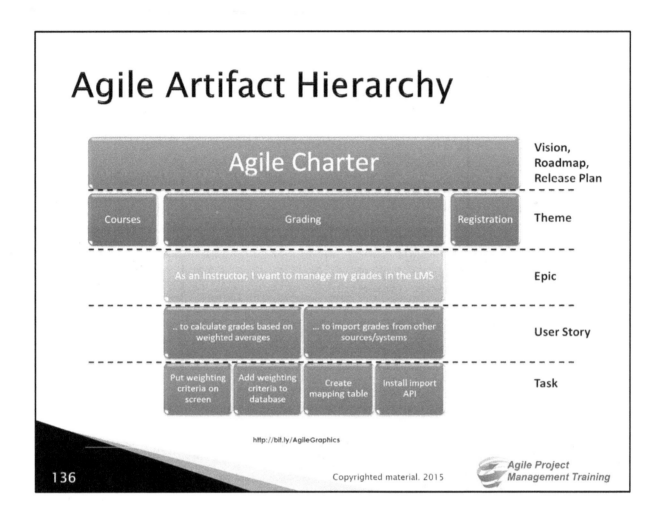

Copyrighted material. 2015

Agile Project Management Training

Notes:

Developing a Vision

- The product vision is key to the success of the project.
- The product vision should align with the company vision
- The vision should be revisited frequently
- All releases of the product should related back to the vision

137   Copyrighted material. 2015

Agile Project Management Training

Notes:

A Product Vision Example

▸ The Learning Management System (LMS) application will give students and faculty access to their courses, content, and grading and will allow them to participate in an online learning community on their desktop and variety of mobile devices.

138

Copyrighted material. 2015

Agile Project
Management Training

Notes:

A Product Roadmap

- High level themes for the next few releases
- Shows progress towards strategy
- Lots of "wiggle room"
- Example:
  1. Implement course listing functionality
  2. Implement grading functionality
  3. Implement discussion groups
  4. Implement student profiles

139

Copyrighted material. 2015

Agile Project Management Training

Notes:

| |
| |
| |
| |
| |
| |
| |
| |

A Release Plan

- ▸ Goes into next level of detail
- ▸ Sets a common understanding
- ▸ A projection, not a commitment
- ▸ Example
  - ◦ Release 1:
    - · LMS Installed with pilot group logins validated
    - · Pilot with 3 faculty and 60 students
    - · Course listings available
  - ◦ Release 2
    - · Incorporate pilot feedback
    - · Enable College of Engineering faculty and students
    - · Implement course selection on-line
  - ◦ Release 3
    - · ...

140

Copyrighted material. 2015

Agile Project Management Training

Copyrighted material. 2015

Notes:

Copyrighted material. 2015

Agile Project
Management Training

Notes:

Requirements Management in Agile

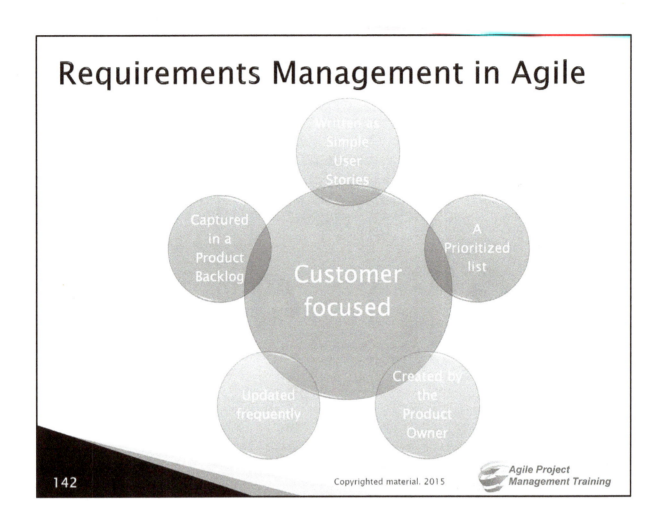

Copyrighted material. 2015

*Agile Project
Management Training*

Notes:

Types of Backlogs

Type	Definition
Product Backlog	Set of prioritized requirements which align with the product vision
Release Backlog	The minimum requirements that would support a release.

Copyrighted material. 2015

Agile Project Management Training

Copyrighted material. 2015

Notes:

Copyrighted material. 2015

Agile Project
Management Training

Notes:

Agile Requirements – User Stories

- A User Story is a very high-level definition of a requirement.
- Agreement between customer and developer to have a conversation.
- User Stories are one of the primary development artifacts for Scrum and Extreme Programming (XP) project teams.
- They contain just enough information to produce a reasonable estimate of the effort to implement it.

145

Copyrighted material. 2015

 *Agile Project Management Training*

Notes:

Themes , Epics and User Stories

Themes
- Themes are groups of related stories. Often the stories all contribute to a common goal or are related in some obvious way, such as all focusing on a single function.

Epics
- Epics resemble themes in the sense that they are made up of multiple stories. As opposed to themes, however, these stories often comprise a complete workflow for a user.

User Stories
- A User story is a self-contained unit of work agreed upon by the developers and the stakeholders. Stories are the building blocks of your release plan.

146

Copyrighted material. 2015

Agile Project Management Training

Notes:

Themes, Epics and User Stories

Grading	Theme
As an Instructor, I want to manage my grades in the LMS	Epic
.. to calculate grades based on weighted averages ... to import grades from other sources/systems	User Story
Put weighting criteria on screen Add weighting criteria to database Create mapping table Install import API	Task

Copyrighted material. 2015

Agile Project Management Training

Notes:

Product Backlog Creation: Writing User Stories

> As a (role), I want (goal/desire)
> *or*
> As a (role), I want (goal/desire) so that (benefit)

- As a user, I want to search for employees by their first and last names.
- As an administrator, I want to be able to reset passwords for any user so that I can help them if they lose their password.

Copyrighted material. 2015

Agile Project Management Training

148

Notes:

Kanban Cards

- In manufacturing, Kanban is defined as "a card containing a set of manufacturing specifications and requirements, used to regulate the supply of components."
- In software, it serves a similar function.
- The card show a backlog item written as a requirement or user story. As a task is completed, it is moved through the Kanban board to show progress and regulate work.
- Kanban does not prescribe a format. The follow pages show Kanban Cards using User Stories.

149

Copyrighted material. 2015

Agile Project Management Training

Notes:

A Kanban Card with User Story Format – Front

Priority:		Size:

As a:

I want to:(what)

So that: (why)

Started:	Due:	Competed:

Copyrighted material. 2015

Agile Project
Management Training

Notes:

A Kanban Card with User Story Format – Back

Key Tasks	Revised Estimate:

Analysis:

Design:

Develop:

Deploy:

Copyrighted material. 2015

Agile Project
Management Training

Notes:

Priority:	Size:

As a:

I want to:(what)

So that: (why)

Started:	Due:	Competed:

Key Tasks	Revised Estimate:

Analysis:

Design:

Develop:

Deploy:

Why use User Stories?

- Emphasizes verbal communication
- Understood by everyone
- Encourages deferring detail
- Supports opportunistic development
- Encourages participatory design

153   Copyrighted material. 2015

Agile Project
Management Training

Notes:

| |
| |
| |
| |
| |
| |
| |
| |

Writing Stories

- Product Owner writes stories on behalf of customer
  - Written in the language of business to allow prioritization
  - Customer is the primary product visionary
- Good stories are:
  - Independent
  - Negotiable
  - Valuable to users or customers
  - Estimable
  - Small
  - Testable   (INVEST)
- Effective Stories are written by role

154

Copyrighted material. 2015

 Agile Project
Management Training

Notes:

Independent

- Stories that depend on other stories are difficult to prioritize and estimate
- Dependent Story:
  - As a user, I want to be able to log in and update my profile
- Independent Stories
  - As a user, I want to be able to log in
  - As a user, I want the ability to update my profile

Copyrighted material. 2015

Agile Project Management Training

Notes:

Negotiable

- ▸ User Stories serve as reminders not contracts
- ▸ Details should be elaborated in conversation
- ▸ User Stories should have a phrase or sentence to serve as reminder to have conversation and should then capture notes about conversation

156

Copyrighted material. 2015

Agile Project Management Training

Notes:

Why not User Stories?

- It is often difficult to understand the relationship between stories
- Not suitable for requirements traceability (if required by process)
- Difficult scaling to large teams
- Certain technical User Stories do not lend themselves to this format;
  - e.g. *As a DBA I need to update the database to the next version of SQL to maintain the license.* – clear, but unnecessary

157

Copyrighted material. 2015

Agile Project Management Training

Notes:

Valuable

- Both to people using the software and paying for the software
- Avoid stories valued only by developers (make the benefits to customers/users apparent for these stories)
- Example
  - "All connections to the database are through a connection pool" could be rewritten as "As a System Administrator, I want up to 50 users to be able to use the application with a 5-user database license so that we can reduce the license cost."

158

Copyrighted material. 2015

Agile Project Management Training

Notes:

Examples of specifying value to users

- Good:
  - "A user can search for jobs"
  - "A company can post new jobs"
- Bad:
  - "The software will be written in C++"
  - "The data elements should be added to sysdb"

159

Copyrighted material. 2015

Agile Project Management Training

Notes:

Estimable

Developers should be able to create a relative estimate only be the words on the card.

▸ 3 common reasons why a story might not be estimable

1. Not enough information or team lacks domain knowledge
   ◦ Get additional details from customer

2. New technology or not enough knowledge in the team
   ◦ Perform a spike to explore technology. A spike is a small story or task to research the complexity and effort needed to develop the user story

3. Story is too big
   ◦ Split the story into smaller ones

Copyrighted material. 2015

 Agile Project Management Training

Notes:

Small

- Easy to use in planning
- Split compound & complex stories (Epics)
- Combine too small stories

Copyrighted material. 2015

Agile Project
Management Training

Notes:

| |
| |
| |
| |
| |
| |
| |
| |

Small: Sizing Stories

- Too broad = impossible to test/code, split stories
- Too narrow = more time spent specifying than implementing
- Aim for test & code cycle of about 4 hours to 2 weeks by one or 2 programmers per story
- Split long stories ("epics") into smaller pieces
- Rather than specify small details, get those in conversations with customer & annotate story
- Big stories can serve as placeholders for areas of the system that still need to be discussed

162

Copyrighted material. 2015

Agile Project Management Training

Notes:

Small: Splitting Stories

- ▸ Compound Stories
  - ◦ Conversations may reveal multiple stories
  - ◦ Split along Create/Update/Delete
  - ◦ Split along data boundaries
- ▸ Complex Stories
  - ◦ Split into spikes and develop the new feature stories (define timebox for each spike)
- ▸ Make sure each split-off portion is a good story (INVEST)

Copyrighted material. 2015

Agile Project Management Training

163

Notes:

Testable

- Can't tell if story is "done" without tests
- Create Acceptance Tests
  - Use tests to track details
  - Write the tests before coding
  - Acceptance tests are ideally created by the Product Owner
  - Does not replace unit tests
  - Often written on the back of the User Story card
- Aim for most tests to be automated

Copyrighted material. 2015

Agile Project
Management Training

164

Notes:

Write User Stories by Role

- Brainstorm an initial set of user roles
- Organize the initial set
- Consolidate roles
- Refine the roles
- Prioritize by role

Copyrighted material. 2015

Agile Project
Management Training

165

Notes:

Attributes worth considering when defining roles

- ‣ Frequency with which user will use software
- ‣ User's level of expertise with domain
- ‣ User's general level of proficiency with computers and software
- ‣ User's level of proficiency with this software
- ‣ User's general goal for using software

Copyrighted material. 2015

 Agile Project Management Training

Notes:

Additional User Modeling

- Identify personas
  - Fictitious users
  - Should be described sufficiently so everyone on team feels like they know this "person"
  - Choose personas that truly represent user population
- Identify extreme personas
  - Define users who are going to stress the system

Copyrighted material. 2015

Agile Project Management Training

167

Notes:

Discussion

Who are the extreme personas for your system?

Copyrighted material. 2015

*Agile Project
Management Training*

Gathering Stories: Tools and Techniques

- ‣ User interviews
- ‣ Prototyping
- ‣ Questionnaires
- ‣ Observation
- ‣ Story-writing workshops

Copyrighted material. 2015

Agile Project
Management Training

169

Notes:

Guidelines for Good Stories

- Start with goals, themes or epics
- Size your story appropriately for the time frame it may be implemented in
- Don't rely solely on stories if they can be better expressed in other ways
- Include user roles in stories rather than saying "user"
- Write for a single user ("A Job Seeker" not "Job Seekers")

170

Copyrighted material. 2015

Agile Project Management Training

Notes:

Story Flaws

- Stories are too small
- Interdependent stories
- Goldplating
- Too Many details
- Thinking too far ahead
- Splitting too many stories

Copyrighted material. 2015

Agile Project
Management Training

Notes:

| |
| |
| |
| |
| |
| |
| |
| |

Group Exercise

Evaluate User Stories

Determine which stories do not meet the criteria of INVEST

172

Copyrighted material. 2015

Agile Project
Management Training

Notes:

User Story Examples: LMS Project

Epic 1 Document Management and Editing		Good/Bad
As a Faculty Member, I want...	assignments submitted via the LMS to be searched for direct quotes, so that I can identify students and work with plagiarism.	
As a Faculty Member, I want...	the first release to be in 4 months so that I can use it in the Fall semester	
As a Faculty Member, I want...	to download completed assignments directly to my computer, so that I can edit files outside the LMS.	
As a Faculty Member, I want...	to ensure the Helvetica is part of the font set since it is the most readable font	
As a Student, I want...	to wait to deploy this software until after I graduate so that I don't have to learn something new	
As a Student, I want...	to save content from the LMS as a PDF, so I can protect my content from editing.	
As a Student, I want...	to export the content of a discussion, so that I can view, edit and save in a word processing application on my desktop.	
As the Department Head	I want the deployment of document management to be on time and on budget so that I get my bonus	
Epic 2 Communications		
As a Faculty Member, I want...	to identify specific discussion forum posts, so that I can grade the student responses.	
As a Faculty Member, I want...	to be notified whenever a new message is posted to a discussion I am subscribed to, so that I don't have to enter the LMS to check for each topic's updates.	
As a Student, I want to...	view in one place all classmates that have contributed to a project, document activity, so that I can see what has been done and by whom.	
As a Student, I want to...	view all assignments and due dates for a course in one place, so that I can identify what I need to do and when across the course.	

©2015 Cape Project Management, Inc.

User Story Examples: LMS Project (cont'd)

As a Student, I want to...	see who else is online across the LMS, so I can communicate with classmates and faculty in real time.	
As a Student, I want to...	to post profile information about me, so other students and faculty can know more about each other.	
Epic 3 Assessment & Grading		
As a Faculty Member, I want...	to import exams/assessments and exam questions from external sources (e.g. as MS-Word documents), so that I don't have to reenter them in the LMS.	
As a Faculty Member, I want...	I want the LMS to be easy to use so that I get good evaluations	
As a Faculty Member, I want...	to calculate grades based on weighted averages, so that students always know their standing in the course.	
As a Faculty Member, I want...	to allow individual students to view individual grades, so that students can see their grades per assignment.	
As a Faculty Member, I want...	to export grades in standard and popular file/exchange formats, so I can use external applications to manage my grades.	
As a Student, I want to...	the option of showing everyone's grades in the class anonymously, so that students can compare their grades with the rest of the class.	
As a Student, I want to...	view all of my grades across all courses, so I so not need to enter each course.	
As a Student, I want to...	I want the courses to be easy so that I don't fail	
As a Trainer, I want...	to use secure exam tools so that I can administer exam to both online and in-person students.	
As a Trainer, I want...	I want the training to be engaging so that the class doesn't fall asleep	

©2015 Cape Project Management, Inc.

Agile Sizing and Estimating

- Assumes all traditional estimates are inaccurate
- Focuses on rapid/order of magnitude estimating
- There are two main components of Agile Estimating:
  - Estimation of Size: A high-level estimate for each work item based upon the complexity is created using a neutral unit of measurement called "Story Points." Size is always estimated relative to other stories.
  - Estimation of Effort: The amount of work that can be accomplished based upon the capacity of the team.

Copyrighted material. 2015

Agile Project Management Training

175

Notes:

Relative Sizing using Story Points

- Size is easier to estimate than duration
- Estimates work by comparing User Stories
- Eliminates hours, dollars, and even people from the estimate

Copyrighted material. 2015

Agile Project Management Training

176

Notes:

| |
| |
| |
| |
| |
| |
| |
| |

Sizing Using Hours versus Points

- A Story point is a universal measurement across the team. It is not biased by the experience or skills or any individual on the team.
- Over time, the team reaches a rhythm and it becomes easier for the team to quickly estimate the product backlog.
- Mike Cohn* is big on breaking User Stories down into tasks, which are then estimated in hours.
- Mature teams often convert the points to hours once they have a rhythm. This is key for budgeting releases and contracting with customers.
- There is no "right" answer, just be consistent

*Author of Use Stories Applied, 2004

Agile Project
Management Training

177

Copyrighted material. 2015

Notes:

Story Point Estimating Technique: Planning Poker

- The size is the face value of the card, Jack=15, Queen = 20, King = 25 and Ace = 50.
- Benchmark an average size story first and assign it a 6. (write it on the User Story)
- Each story is given a card relative to the average: bigger, smaller, same.
- Play poker on each story until all team members agree on the size with no more than a variance of 1
- When there is a difference, choose the higher number for the estimate.

http://planningpoker.com/

178   Copyrighted material. 2015

Agile Project
Management Training

Notes:

Agile Estimating Techniques: Fibonacci Sequence

- 0 1 1 2 3 5 8 13 21 34 55...
- Provides more flexibility for unknown larger stories
- Find your smallest story and give it a 1
- Limit the largest number
- Use index cards and estimate similar to planning poker

Copyrighted material. 2015

Agile Project
Management Training

179

Notes:

Group Exercise

Play Planning Poker

Size each story

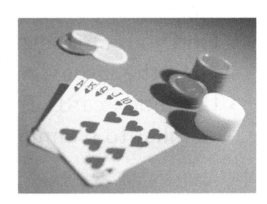

Copyrighted material. 2015

Agile Project
Management Training

Notes:

Estimate User Stories: LMS Project

As a	I want	Size
Faculty Member	assignments submitted via the LMS to be searched for direct quotes, so that I can identify students and work with plagiarism.	
Faculty Member	to download completed assignments directly to my computer, so that I can edit files outside the LMS.	
Student	to wait to deploy this software until after I graduate so that I don't have to learn something new	
Student	to save content from the LMS as a PDF, so I can protect my content from editing.	
Student	to export the content of a discussion, so that I can view, edit and save in a word processing application on my desktop.	
Faculty Member	to identify specific discussion forum posts, so that I can grade the student responses.	
Faculty Member	to be notified whenever a new message is posted to a discussion I am subscribed to, so that I don't have to enter the LMS to check for each topic's updates.	
Student	view in one place all classmates that have contributed to a project, document activity, so that I can see what has been done and by whom.	
Student	view all assignments and due dates for a course in one place, so that I can identify what I need to do and when across the course.	
Student	see who else is online across the LMS, so I can communicate with classmates and faculty in real time.	
Student	to post profile information about me, so other students and faculty can know more about each other.	
Faculty Member	to import exams/assessments and exam questions from external sources (e.g. as MS-Word documents), so that I don't have to reenter them in the LMS.	
Faculty Member	to calculate grades based on weighted averages, so that students always know their standing in the course.	
Faculty Member	to allow individual students to view individual grades, so that students can see their grades per assignment.	
Faculty Member	to export grades in standard and popular file/exchange formats, so I can use external applications to manage my grades.	
Student	the option of showing everyone's grades in the class anonymously, so that students can compare their grades with the rest of the class.	
Student	view all of my grades across all courses, so I so not need to enter each course.	

©2015 Cape Project Management, Inc.

Prioritization

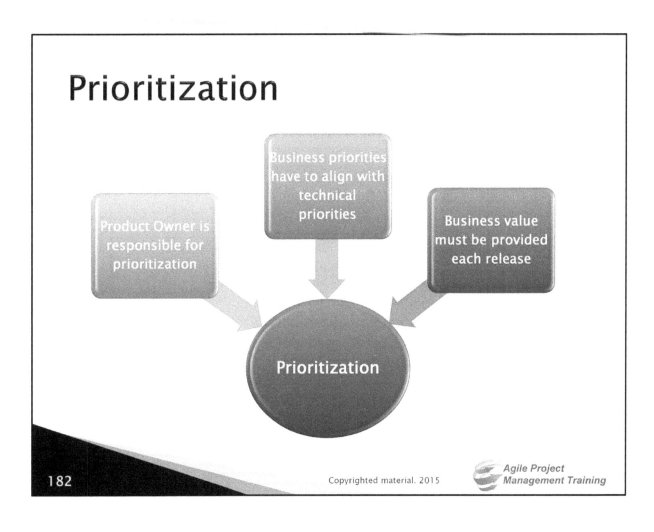

Copyrighted material. 2015

Agile Project
Management Training

Notes:

Prioritization Techniques

- Cumulative voting (the money game)
- Critical, important, useful categories
- Pair-wise comparison

Copyrighted material. 2015

Agile Project
Management Training

Notes:

| |
| |
| |
| |
| |
| |
| |

Group Exercise

Prioritize User Stories

Prioritize each user story by Critical, Important, Useful.

Copyrighted material. 2015

Agile Project
Management Training

184

Notes:

Prioritize User Stories: LMS Project

As a	I want	Critical Important Useful
Faculty Member	assignments submitted via the LMS to be searched for direct quotes, so that I can identify students and work with plagiarism.	
Faculty Member	to download completed assignments directly to my computer, so that I can edit files outside the LMS.	
Student	to wait to deploy this software until after I graduate so that I don't have to learn something new	
Student	to save content from the LMS as a PDF, so I can protect my content from editing.	
Student	to export the content of a discussion, so that I can view, edit and save in a word processing application on my desktop.	
Faculty Member	to identify specific discussion forum posts, so that I can grade the student responses.	
Faculty Member	to be notified whenever a new message is posted to a discussion I am subscribed to, so that I don't have to enter the LMS to check for each topic's updates.	
Student	view in one place all classmates that have contributed to a project, document activity, so that I can see what has been done and by whom.	
Student	view all assignments and due dates for a course in one place, so that I can identify what I need to do and when across the course.	
Student	see who else is online across the LMS, so I can communicate with classmates and faculty in real time.	
Student	to post profile information about me, so other students and faculty can know more about each other.	
Faculty Member	to import exams/assessments and exam questions from external sources (e.g. as MS-Word documents), so that I don't have to reenter them in the LMS.	
Faculty Member	to calculate grades based on weighted averages, so that students always know their standing in the course.	
Faculty Member	to allow individual students to view individual grades, so that students can see their grades per assignment.	
Faculty Member	to export grades in standard and popular file/exchange formats, so I can use external applications to manage my grades.	
Student	the option of showing everyone's grades in the class anonymously, so that students can compare their grades with the rest of the class.	
Student	view all of my grades across all courses, so I so not need to enter each course.	

©2015 Cape Project Management, Inc.

Copyrighted material. 2015

Agile Project
Management Training

186

Notes:

Quality Control in Agile

- Creating a Definition of "Done" promotes quality
- Technical debt is more prevalent on Agile projects due to frequent delivery expectations
- Continuous improvement is needed—similar to Six Sigma approach
- Product Owner should be the single owner of quality decisions

Copyrighted material. 2015

Agile Project Management Training

Notes:

Definition of "Done"

- The term "Definition of Done" created by Scrum but is suited well for Kanban as a gating factor to get into the "Done" column.
- Contain the common list of sub-tasks (coding comments, acceptance testing release notes, design documents, etc.) which supports the expected business value fro every release.
- Eliminates the need for additional columns on the Kanban board for every sub-task.
- The intention is to focus on value-added steps that allow the team to focus on what must be completed in order to build software while eliminating wasteful activities.
- The definition of "Done" is defined by the Product Owner and Development Team.
- Make "Done" more stringent over time with each release

Copyrighted material. 2015

Agile Project
Management Training

Notes:

Technical Debt

- Development decisions made in the short term which cause more work in the long-term
- Not necessarily apparent to the user
- Meets test cases and is not a defect
- Major challenge of Agile

189

Copyrighted material. 2015

Agile Project
Management Training

Notes:

| |
| |
| |
| |
| |
| |
| |
| |

Technical Debt

	Reckless	Prudent
Deliberate	"We don't have time for design"	"We will have to ship and deal with consequences"
Inadvertent	"I thought this was just a Proof of Concept"	"Now we know how we should have built it"

Copyrighted material. 2015

Agile Project Management Training

Notes:

Managing Technical Debt

- Ensure coding standards and unit testing
- Enforce code reviews
- Refactor code when possible
- Quantify effort to Product Owner
- Consider pair-programming
- Pursue continuous integration
- Commit to a well-defined Definition of Done

191

Copyrighted material. 2015

Agile Project Management Training

Notes:

Implementing Kanban

Copyrighted material. 2015

Agile Project
Management Training

Implementing Kanban

▸ David Anderson, a Kanban thought-leader, suggests that Kanban Implementations are based on 3 principles*:

1. Start with what you do now
2. Agree to pursue incremental, evolutionary change
3. Initially, respect current processes, roles, responsibilities & job titles

*http://www.djaa.com/principles-kanban-method-0

Copyrighted material. 2015

Agile Project
Management Training

Notes:

Start with what you do now

- The Kanban Method does not ask you to change your existing process.
- It is based on the concept that you evolve your current process.
- There is no sweeping, engineered change to a new process definition or style of working.

194

Copyrighted material. 2015

 Agile Project
Management Training

Notes:

Agree to pursue incremental, evolutionary change

- The organization (or team) must agree that their current circumstances warrant an evolutionary approach to improvement.
- Recent failures or politics of the organization may make it too risky for managers to propose and implement sweeping changes.
- Without agreement that a slow, evolutionary, incremental approach is the right way forward then there may not be the right environment or management support for a Kanban initiative.

195   Copyrighted material. 2015

Agile Project Management Training

Notes:

Respect the current process, roles, responsibilities and job titles

▸ Most organizations have elements that work acceptably and are worth preserving.

▸ By agreeing to respect current roles, responsibilities and job titles we eliminate initial fears.

▸ This should enable us to gain broader support for our Kanban initiative.

196

Copyrighted material. 2015

Agile Project Management Training

Notes:

"We are what we repeatedly do. Excellence then, is not an act, but a habit."

Aristotle

Copyrighted material. 2015

*Agile Project
Management Training*

Notes:

Implementation Steps

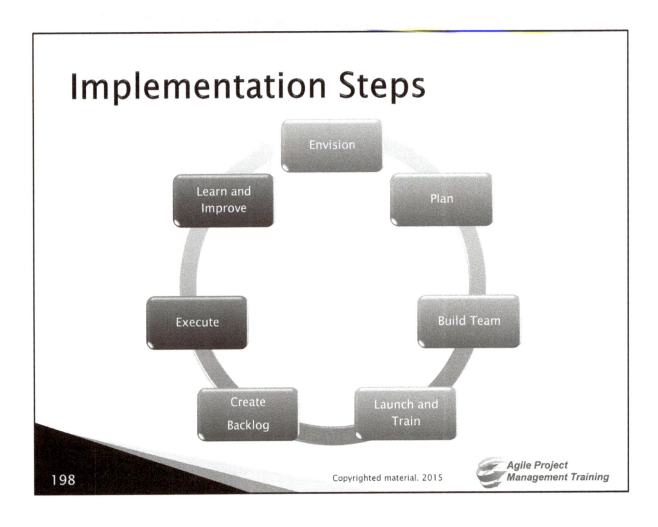

Copyrighted material. 2015

Agile Project
Management Training

198

Notes:

Envision

- ‣ Find a champion or sponsor
  - ◦ C Level executive
  - ◦ IT Manager
  - ◦ Project or program manager
- ‣ Start with an urgent and very important project
  - ◦ Preferably one that is struggling with "typical" problems
  - ◦ Don't be afraid to oversell
- ‣ Involve middle management

199

Copyrighted material. 2015

Agile Project Management Training

Notes:

Plan

- Don't over think the implementation.
- Brainstorm with the team the initial process changes they want to implement:
- Phase I
  - Kanban Board
  - Kanban Cards
  - Bi-weekly Retrospectives
- Phase II
  - More or less columns
  - Clarity on Cycle Times
  - Advanced reporting
- Allow the plan to evolve

Copyrighted material. 2015

Agile Project
Management Training

200

Notes:

Build the Right Team

Have the right people – get the risk–takers:
- ▸ Willing to learn new habits
- ▸ Willing to be pioneers
- ▸ Enthusiastic about Agile and Kanban
- ▸ 100% committed to the team

Copyrighted material. 2015

Agile Project
Management Training

Notes:

Launch and Train

- Perform a Kanban launch meeting/immersion
- Include Kanban training
- Introduce and practice self-organizing team concepts
- Let the team identify initial roadblocks and how to overcome them

Copyrighted material. 2015

202

Notes:

Create Backlog

- Sell Kanban to the business
- Find a superior product owner
- Create and align the product backlog to company goals and objectives
- Train the business on product prioritization
- Create an initial release plan

203

Copyrighted material. 2015

Agile Project
Management Training

Notes:

Execute

- ▸ Define "Done"
- ▸ Begin work on backlog Items
- ▸ Hold Daily Standups
- ▸ Utilize all Kanban techniques you have planned for.
- ▸ First month is often called Phase 0

204

Copyrighted material. 2015

Notes:

Inspect and Adapt – Phase 0

▸ Hold a longer than typical retrospective since there will have been many observations within the first month.

▸ Perform the following:
  ◦ Happiness Metric with Kanban
  ◦ Review cycle time and lessons learned for roadblocks or idle time
  ◦ Discuss process improvement opportunities
  ◦ Have fun! Celebrate the success of trying something new.

Copyrighted material. 2015

Agile Project Management Training

205

Notes:

Prepare for Change

- Communicate business drivers for change to Kanban. They can include:
  - Less willing to invest in long term development
  - Critical mass of successful case studies
  - Speed to market or customer satisfaction.
- Don't underestimate the impact of change
- Be prepared to respond to resistance
- With Kanban, you don't need a "big-bang" change, you can slowly introduce the change to the organization.

206

Copyrighted material. 2015

Agile Project Management Training

Notes:

Types of Change

Developmental	· Improvements on processes, methods or performance standards · These are done in order to stay competitive · Causes little stress to employees
Transitional	· More intrusive because it introduces something completely new · Examples are re-organization, mergers, acquisition, new technology · May cause instability and insecurity
Transformational	· Occurs after the transition period · Transformation may be necessary when there are radical changes within or outside of the company

Copyrighted material. 2015

Agile Project Management Training

Notes:

Dealing with Resistance: What to Do

☑ Explain the reasons behind the change
☑ Identify the advantages
☑ Be open for questions
☑ Set standards and clear targets
☑ Encourage participation and early involvement
☑ Recognize and reward efforts
☑ Encourage self-management
☑ Stimulate creative thinking
☑ Seek opportunities the change may bring about

208

Copyrighted material. 2015

Agile Project Management Training

Notes:

Dealing with Resistance: What <u>Not</u> to Do

- ⊘ Avoid the individual
- ⊘ Lose your confidence
- ⊘ Use aggressive language
- ⊘ Give too many excuses
- ⊘ Threaten
- ⊘ Expect immediate approval or support
- ⊘ Expect to have all the answers at once
- ⊘ Fight with the people resisting
- ⊘ Be obsessive with the details

209

Copyrighted material. 2015

Agile Project Management Training

Notes:

5 Basic Principles of Change Management

People react differently to change.

Everyone has basic needs that have to be met or fulfilled.

Expectations must be managed sensibly.

Fears have to be dealt with.

Change often involves loss or grief and people go through the grief cycle or the change curve.

Copyrighted material. 2015

Agile Project Management Training

210

Notes:

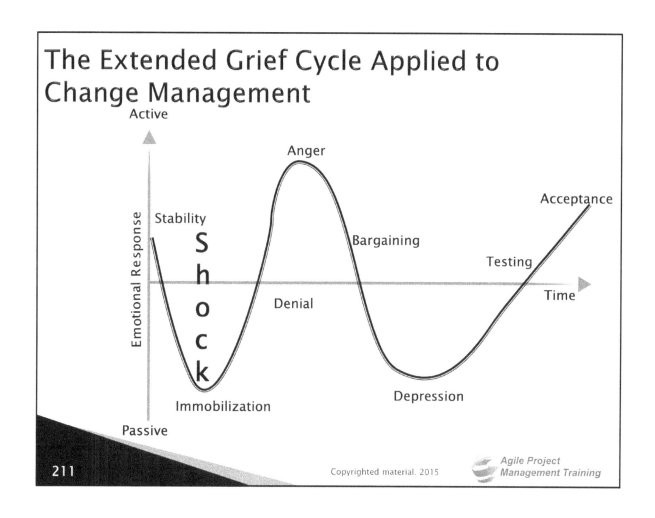

The Extended Grief Cycle Applied to Change Management

Copyrighted material. 2015

Agile Project Management Training

211

Notes:

Discussion

Where is your organization?

Copyrighted material. 2015

 Agile Project Management Training

Notes:

Reasons Why Change Efforts Fail

- Inability to identify all the urgent reasons for change
- Failure to point out the one crucial reason for change
- Lack of commitment
- Lack of determination
- Unsuccessful strategizing, execution and comprehension
- Lack of follow through and control
- Impatience to see immediate results
- Inability to adapt and be flexible
- Resistance overpowers the need to change
- Fear

213

Copyrighted material. 2015

Agile Project Management Training

Notes:

Kotter – 8 Steps to Successful Change

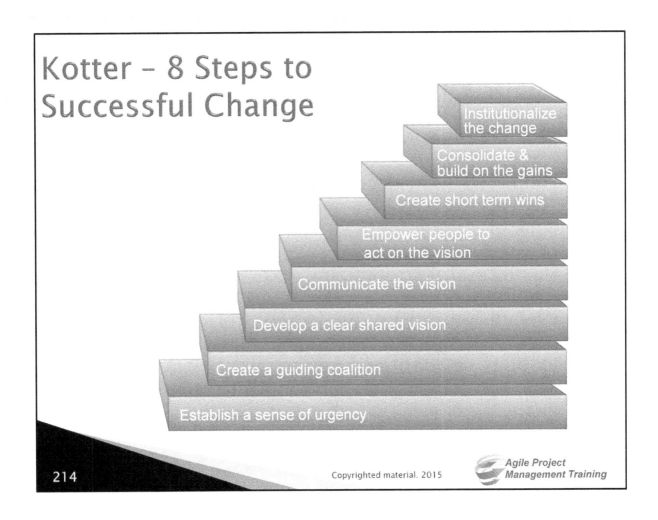

- Institutionalize the change
- Consolidate & build on the gains
- Create short term wins
- Empower people to act on the vision
- Communicate the vision
- Develop a clear shared vision
- Create a guiding coalition
- Establish a sense of urgency

214

Copyrighted material. 2015

Agile Project Management Training

Notes:

"We are what we repeatedly do. Excellence then, is not an act, but a habit."

Aristotle

Copyrighted material. 2015

Agile Project
Management Training

Notes:

Forces of Change

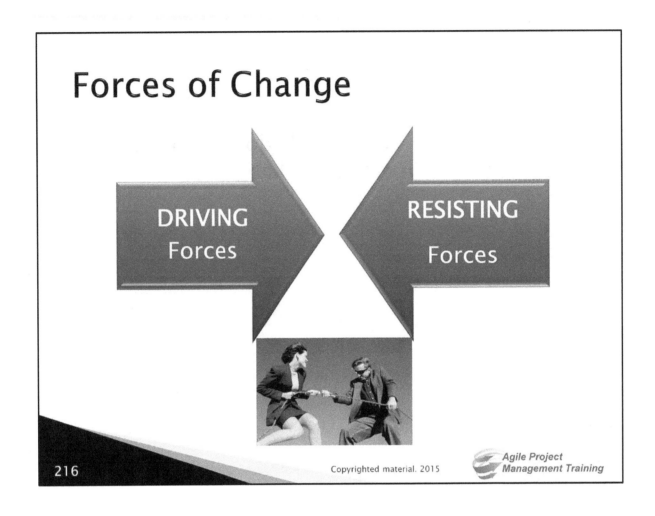

Copyrighted material. 2015

Agile Project
Management Training

216

Notes:

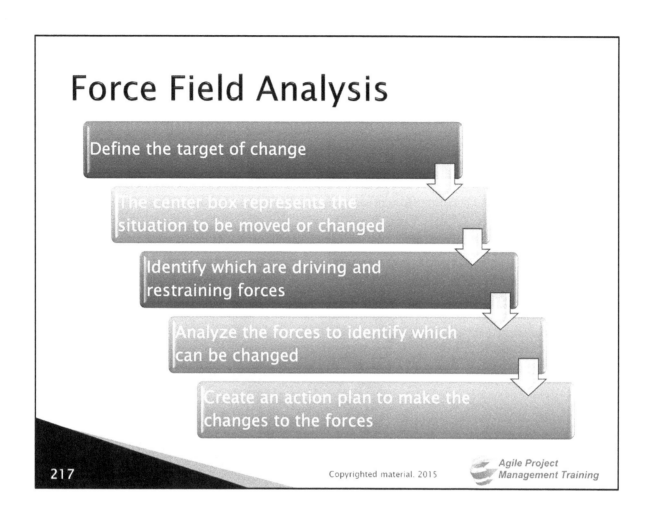

Copyrighted material. 2015

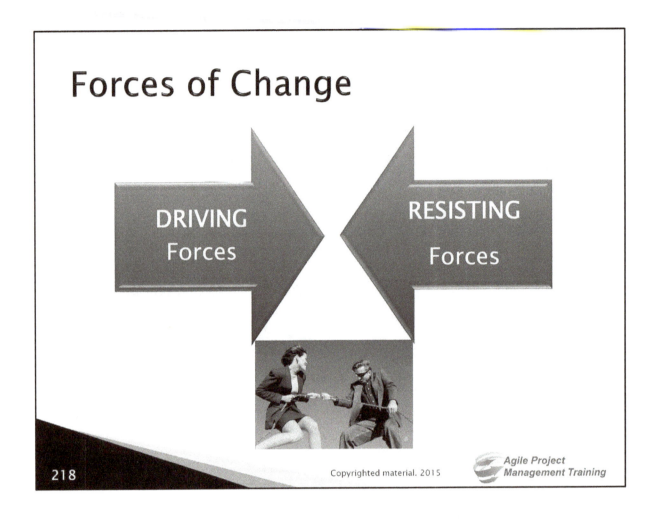

Forces of Change

DRIVING Forces

RESISTING Forces

Copyrighted material. 2015

Agile Project
Management Training

218

Notes:

Force Field Analysis

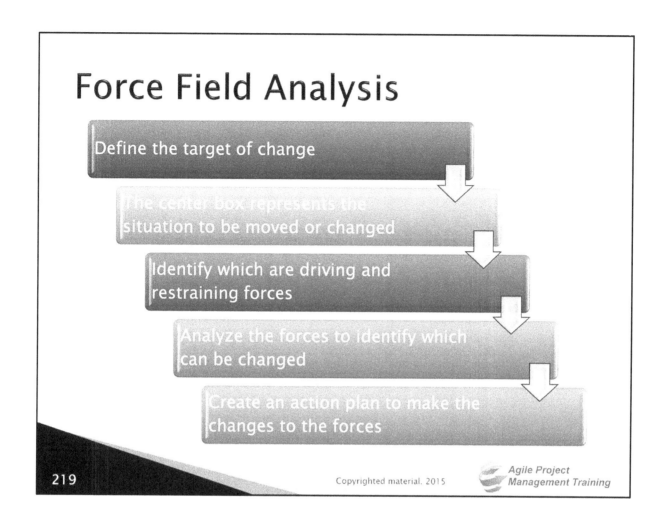

Define the target of change

The center box represents the situation to be moved or changed

Identify which are driving and restraining forces

Analyze the forces to identify which can be changed

Create an action plan to make the changes to the forces

219

Copyrighted material. 2015

Agile Project Management Training

Notes:

Activity

Force Field Analysis

220

Copyrighted material. 2015

Agile Project
Management Training

Copyrighted material. 2015

Notes:

Force Field Analysis

Directions

1. Use the worksheet on the next page.

2. On the center box, write taking change you are anticipating.

3. List all the forces FOR CHANGE in one column, and all the forces AGAINST CHANGE in another column.

4. Rate the strength of these forces and assign a numerical weight, 1 being the weakest, 5 being the strongest.

5. When you add the "strength points" of the forces, you'll see the viability of the proposed change.

The tool can be used to help ensure the success of the proposed change by identifying the strength of the forces against the change.

ACTIVITY SHEET: *Force Field Analysis*

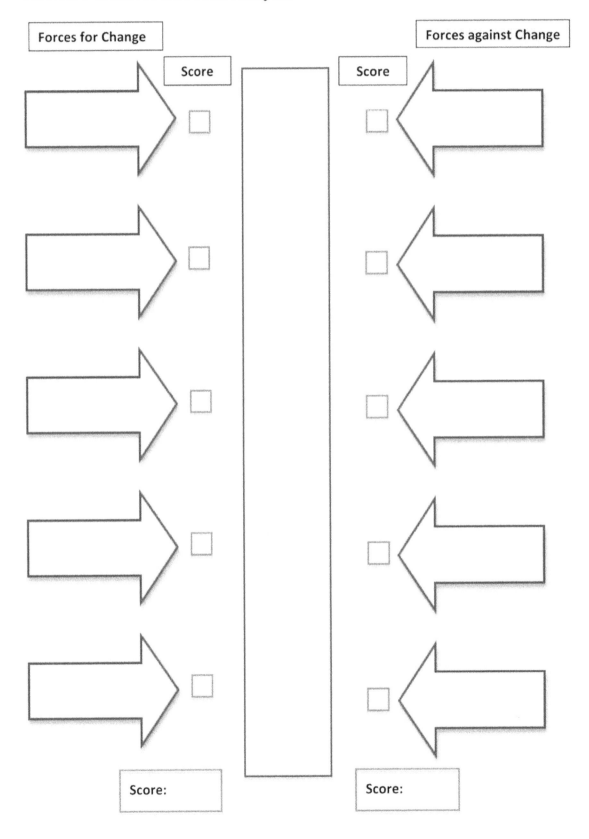

Kanban is "Easy"

‣ Minimal process overhead
‣ Less bureaucracy
‣ Less documentation
‣ Less surprises

223

Copyrighted material. 2015

Agile Project
Management Training

Notes:

Kanban is Hard

- Change in processes
- Change in bureaucracy
- Change in standards
- Different kinds of surprises

"When you're finished changing, you're finished."

– Benjamin Franklin

Copyrighted material. 2015

Agile Project Management Training

224

Notes:

Key to Success:
Change the Paradigm

- ‣ Admit what you did before wasn't working; do something different
- ‣ The only measure of success is delivered software
- ‣ Move from micromanagement to trust
- ‣ Don't punish risk-taking or failure

Copyrighted material. 2015

Agile Project Management Training

225

Notes:

Activity

Day 2 Agile Review Game
http://bit.ly/AgileGames

Copyrighted material. 2015

Agile Project
Management Training

226

Notes:

Thank-You!

227

Copyrighted material. 2015

Agile Project
Management Training

Additional References

In addition to specific references noted on slides, general references are below:

‣ Ken Schwaber and Jeff Sutherland. 2013. The Scrum Guide. http://www.Scrumguides.org and is licensed under a Creative Commons: http://creativecommons.org/licenses/by-sa/4.0/.

‣ Mike Cohn. http://www.mountaingoatsoftware.com/blog/why-i-dont-use-story-points-for-sprint-planning

‣ The Scrum Master Competency model was adapted from original source: http://www.slideshare.net/fullscreen/smithcdau/agile-coaching-workshop-13180108/15

‣ The online Agile self-assessment was adapted from original source developed by Henrik Kniberg and is licensed under a Creative Commons: http://creativecommons.org/licenses/by-nc-nd/3.0/

‣ Dan Tousignant. http://www.agileprojectmanagementtraining.com/are-you-implementing-scrum-but-realize-you-are-better-suited-for-kanban/

Copyrighted material. 2015

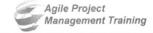

www.ingramcontent.com/pod-product-compliance
Lightning Source LLC
Chambersburg PA
CBHW080405060326
40689CB00019B/4142